# Yugoslavia Dismembered

# Yugoslavia Dismembered

## Catherine Samary
### Translated by Peter Drucker

Monthly Review Press
New York

Copyright © 1995 by Monthly Review Press
All rights reserved

First published in France under the title *La Déchirure yougoslave*,
© 1994 by L'Harmattan

*Library of Congress Cataloging-in-Publication Data*
Samary, Catherine
[Déchirure yougoslave. English]
　　Yugoslavia dismembered / Catherine Samary : translated by Peter Drucker.
　　　　p.　cm.
　　Includes bibliographical references.
　　ISBN 0-85345-921-5 (cloth) — ISBN 0-85345-922-3 (paper)
　　1. Yugoslav War, 1991- —Causes. 2. Nationalism—Yugoslavia.
3. Yugoslavia—Politics and government. 4. Yugoslavia—Ethnic relations. 5. National security—Europe. I. Title.
DR1313.S2613 1995
949.702'4—dc20　　　　　　　　　　　　　　　　　　　95-12971
　　　　　　　　　　　　　　　　　　　　　　　　　　　CIP

Maps on pages 16, 117, and 118 adapted from Robert J. Donia and John V.A. Fine, Jr., *Bosnia and Herzegovina: A Tradition Betrayed* (London: Hurst & Co., 1994).

Monthly Review Press
122 West 27th Street
New York NY 10001

Manufactured in the United States of America

10 9 8 7 6 5 4 3 2 1

For Hubert

*For your sharp criticisms*
*For our fruitful disagreements*
*For everything that I have taken and learned from you*

For Myriam and for Jean

I dedicate this book
to all the men and women who resist,
to my friends—
Serbs, Croats, Slovenes,
Gypsies, Montenegrins, Macedonians,
Muslims, Albanians, Jews—
Bosnians, Yugoslavs, "Eskimos"....*

---

* Many former Yugoslavs who reject nationalist divisions have taken to calling themselves "Eskimos," even on census forms, instead of Serb, Croat, Muslim, etc. The term is meant in an entirely positive sense.

# Contents

*Preface*   9

*Background on Yugoslavia*   15

*Introduction.* The Yugoslav Crisis: An Overview   25

1. Indeterminate Nationalities   35

2. Titoism's Balance Sheet   51

3. Wars Within the War   69

4. The Bosnian Symbol   85

5. The "International Community" on Trial   111

*Conclusion.* Today Yugoslavia;
Tomorrow Europe?   130

*Chronological Appendix*   145
*Notes*   159
*Bibliography*   173
*Index*   179

# Tables

| | |
|---|---|
| Yugoslavia According to the 1981 Census | 15 |
| The Mosaic of Peoples | 17 |
| Ethnic Composition of the Republics | 19 |
| The Yugoslav Crisis: Names | 20 |
| Yugoslavia in Historical Context: Key Dates | 24 |
| Tito's Yugoslavia: Key Dates | 51 |
| Disparities Between Republics | 68 |
| The Yugoslav Crisis: Key Dates | 69 |
| Main Periods in Bosnian History | 85 |
| Ethnic Groups and Religions in Bosnia-Herzegovina | 87 |
| Peace Plans | 116 |

# Maps

| | |
|---|---|
| Tito's Yugoslavia | 16 |
| Ethnic Composition of the Republics | 18 |
| Vance-Owen Plan, January 1993 | 117 |
| Owen-Stoltenberg Plan, August 1993 | 117 |
| Military Fronts, March 1994 | 118 |

# Preface

The "ethnic cleansing" in former Yugoslavia continues. First minority communities are expelled. Then children of mixed marriages are attacked, and all the "bad Serbs," "bad Croats," and "bad Muslims": i.e., everyone who tries to elude the tightening net that hinders any expression of diversity of thought, interest, identity, or political choice. In early 1995 the last independent newspaper in Belgrade was brought into line. Croat extremist newspapers have already denounced "leftists, pacifists, feminists, and homosexuals" as anti-Croat. Children of mixed marriages are described as "bastards" in the Muslim fundamentalist press. Everywhere trade unionists who dare to go on strike against the ruling parties' policies are denounced as "fifth columnists."

Given the horrors of "ethnic cleansing," of course, the idea that communities must be separated from one another keeps winning new converts. Wasn't that the point of the war? This idea will keep the war going, too, openly or covertly, so that each miniature country can increase its *Lebensraum*, so that new miniature countries can be created from other ethnically mixed areas, such as Macedonia—or so that the victims of these oppressive policies can resist.

What is the cause of these tragedies? How much responsibility does each side bear for this disaster; how much responsibility does the "international community" bear?

Political analyses of the conflict—and proposed solutions—are at opposite extremes from one other. The media's images of the war, rather than helping us understand, serve to activate emotional reflexes by making false analogies. On one side, Munich, fascism, and extermination camps are evoked in order to rally support for a military intervention against the new Hitler who supposedly rules in Belgrade. The other side responds pell-mell with Croat Ustashe fascism, the threat of Islamic fundamentalism, and clashes between all the various reactionary nationalisms, in order to advocate *de facto* neutrality in the conflict.

Each side can pick and choose from the reality of the crisis the "undeniable" truths that favor its particular interpretation. For one side, these truths are: secret plans for the creation of Greater Serbia; ethnic cleansing carried out by Serb ("Chetnik") extremists who preach hate; and ethnic separation by means of humiliation, rape, wrecking mosques, razing villages, laying siege to cities, the killings and threats that have made hundreds of thousands of refugees take flight. The other side emphasizes: massive ethnic discrimination in Croatia; Croatian President Franjo Tudjman's revisionist rewriting of history and rehabilitation of old fascists; policies of ethnic cleansing carried out by Croat militias in Bosnia (who destroyed the Muslim neighborhoods of Mostar); Bosnian President Alija Izetbegovic's Islamic Declaration; Islamic fundamentalist currents, supported by Arab countries, on the offensive in Bosnia; and the violence committed on every side.

Selecting one substantial part of reality hides (and may be meant to hide) the rest. One side denies the *joint* responsibility for the war. The other side minimizes the pivotal role of the Serb question and the disastrous Greater Serbia project in setting off this crisis. One side, in order to focus on (and bomb?) its identified target portrays Bosnia's past and its present-day society as an idyll of perfect tolerance and centuries-old stability, destroyed by an outside, Serbian aggressor. In so doing they skip over all the aspects of crisis and polarization that affect Bosnian society itself (including the outside, *Croatian* aggressor), particularly ignoring the cultural and social differentiation between city and countryside and fights for power by Bosnian Serb, Croat, and Muslim nationalist parties. This means that in their eyes a foreign military intervention could save Bosnia, because Bosnia itself is not in crisis—there is only one, "clear" target, and it can be bombed.

The other side by contrast relies on a pseudofatalistic chain of supposedly centuries-old interethnic clashes in order to "explain" the Yugoslav crisis and the break-up of Bosnia. In so doing they avoid analyzing the plans drawn up in Belgrade and Zagreb for the partition of Bosnia or the sieges of ethnically mixed areas where people want to live together.

Neither of these two approaches is convincing, whatever the rational kernel each may contain. They converge in their ignorance of the deep socioeconomic causes of the crisis. Denunciations of "Serb fascism" on one side, or of "interethnic hatred" (or even a "German plot") on the other, makes up for the lack of analysis. The historical analogies they make prevent them from seeing this war's real motive force: "cleansing" territory in order to carve out nation-states.

But above all, these approaches do not make clear the factors that are not narrowly "Yugoslav" in this war, factors that this war has in common with other tragedies that are taking place *today*, elsewhere, particularly in the former Soviet Union. We therefore have to shed light on the *society in crisis* that fosters the nationalism of the "higher-ups" (who wage war over how to divide the cake, with whatever means they have at their disposal) and the nationalism of "ordinary people" (who are afraid of not ending up in the "right country," i.e. the country that would protect their property, their jobs, their identity, their children, and their lives).

The break-up of a multinational country, Yugoslavia, is combined with the crisis of a (socioeconomic and political) system, in the context of a world where the "free market" is on the offensive. In this crisis the Yugoslav communities' past obviously makes a specific difference, and the dark pages of their history are highlighted. But the crisis is *rooted* in the present, chaotic transition from one system of power and property to another. The market and the abolition of redistributive policies have deepened regional divides. Eagerness to join the European Union more quickly made the rich republics Slovenia and Croatia cut loose from the others. The declarations of independence from Yugoslavia aimed particularly at making sure that the selling off of collective resources would benefit the republican governments and their clienteles. This is why the Yugoslav case tells us something about the wars and conflicts in the former Soviet Union and about the break-up of Czechoslovakia.

The free-market policies advocated in the East are a disaster. So why should the "international community"—i.e., the world's most powerful governments—have any legitimacy when they try to impose solutions on the people affected by these policies?

A Yalta II atmosphere prevails in the Balkans: the great powers' (partly divergent) interests count more in the choice of alliances than any analysis of the real causes of the crisis, more than the fate of peoples. What kind of Balkan "order" can be born in this way? The United States has dissociated itself from the European peace plans, but without putting forward a substantially different approach. The "peace plans" proposed for Bosnia-Herzegovina, whether they are signed or not, will not bring stability to the country or the Balkan region as long as they strengthen exclusionary nationalism by ratifying ethnic partition.

Criticizing our rulers' policies only increases the importance of active solidarity "from below" with the victims of this dirty war. Even if analogies with Nazism are open to challenge, that in no way lessens the need for resistance to rising fascistic and racist forces. We must not wait for something on the scale of the Nazi genocide of the Jews before we denounces crimes against humanity, including "ethnic cleansing," *wherever* they take place. Serbian President Slobodan Milosevic does not have to be Hitler for us to fight against reactionary Greater Serbian policies. But we cannot fight Greater Serbian policies effectively as long as we keep silent about Greater Croatian policies.

Defending the multiethnic, multicultural Bosnian society does not require a rosy portrayal of what it really is, still less identification with whoever makes up the Bosnian government. Rejecting the lying equation "Muslim = fundamentalist," which is particularly false in Bosnia-Herzegovina, does not require us to condone fundamentalist currents that the war is fostering, which also threaten multiethnic Bosnia. Defending multiethnic Bosnia does require, urgently, that we avoid any nationalist "demonization" or "homogenization" of any of the Bosnian peoples (e.g., the Serb or Muslim community), a danger that is exacerbated by alliances formed against one particular people (i.e., the Serb-Croat alliance at the Muslim community's expense, or the Croat-Muslim alliance against the Serbs). It is also essential to denounce any purely "ethnic" portrayal of these peoples. As the author wrote in the beginning of 1993:

> If President Izetbegovic is described as representing the third community, the Muslims, then who speaks for besieged Sarajevo and resisting Tuzla? Who represents all the communities that are mixed together in a blend of differences that they claim as a Bosnian identity? Who represents those Bosnians who are in despair at being devoured by the "two demons—one that eats the body and the other that eats the soul"—of Serb and Croat nationalism, which in fact are covertly allied against them? Who represents the Bosnians who know how much denouncing the Croat massacres of Muslims in Prozor will cost the Bosnian refugees in Croatia, because Bosnia's

alliance with the Croatian government means that only one aggressor, the main one, can be named? Who represents those Bosnians who are Muslim in the same way that I'm Jewish: an atheist, "ethnically impure," and proud of it?

Who represents the thousands of Bosnian Serbs (or Serbs elsewhere) who are considered "traitors" to the "Serb national cause" when they resist ethnic cleansing? Who represents the Serbs who sign petitions rejecting the madness of "Greater Serbia"? Who represents the Serbs fighting in the Bosnian army against the policies of Karadzic (leader of the self-declared Serb Republic of Bosnia-Herzegovina), who pretends to express their self-determination through massacres, terrorism, and rapes?

Who represents the Bosnian Croats shoved aside by Tudjman's ruling party because they are "too Bosnian"? Who represents the Croats who reject the acts of Mate Boban, leader of the "self-declared Croat Republic of Herceg-Bosna," who speaks in their name? Who represents the Croats who want to defend Bosnia in a Bosnian uniform—not under a Croatian flag, not in uniforms from which no one has even bothered to unsew the German flag?

Who represents those who feel that they are "Yugoslav," who are today being torn apart?

No one can be allowed to say, "We did not know." Prosecution of all those who commit war crimes, including rape, is morally and politically urgent. The freeing of populations under siege should be a precondition for any political agreement. *But we have to say what we know*, everything *we know*. The distinction between victims and aggressors is necessary. But the distinction becomes perverse if it means not telling the whole truth. (From Catherine Samary's op-ed, "Les mots pour le dire," *Le Monde*, 14 January 1993.)

Two years after this piece was written, three years after the siege of Sarajevo began, the aggressions that are stifling Bosnian society are coming from several sides. They include a current, more and more visibly dissociated from the Bosnian "camp," that advocates an Islamic state: a counsel of despair for some, a fundamentalist choice for others.

So is there still really a multicultural country called "Bosnia" to defend? Yes and no.

*No*, because Bosnian society has been deeply rent and polarized by the war: that was the war's point. Nor is there any government any more that is recognized by all the different Bosnian communities.

Divisions among the nationalist parties that dominate the Bosnian government could still explode the Croat-Muslim federation.

But *yes*, multicultural Bosnia exists—as an alternative project, relying on those who still resist policies of ethnic cleansing not only in Bosnia-Herzegovina but also in Serbia and Croatia. Because Bosnia's future is organically linked to that of its neighbors. A Balkan explosion is still possible if reciprocal (political and socioeconomic) guarantees are not found to enable peoples to live together in this region. This is not a question of percentages of land.

Stopping the fighting is not the same as overcoming the crisis. Once the fighting stops the governments in power will face the key question: *what kind of society can be built that will not compound destruction by war with destruction by an inhuman social order?* The currents that oppose the dominant nationalisms can only offer *social insecurity*, because they accept the predominant neoliberal economic orientation (which makes populist nationalism seem at least a bit more protective by contrast). The free market without frontiers that they generally advocate offers no solutions to the Yugoslav crisis. It has been one of the factors aggravating the crisis.

This disintegrative process will in turn threaten the newly independent countries: new "autonomous republics" and "nations" will continue to spring up. As we can see in all the Eastern European countries, this territorial fragmentation will be compounded by social disintegration, "third-worldization." This is why people are disillusioned—and why governments are unstable in all the Eastern countries.

Free market policies will give birth to new explosions in Europe as it has in Mexico. There will be no peaceful "new world order" founded on exclusion. Antiliberal and fascist nationalism is the "classical" answer to such crises. Isn't it time to invent other answers, on the world scale on which the problems are posed?

*February 1995*

### Acknowledgment

I would like to thank Peter Drucker, not only for his translation but also for his stimulating comments and suggestions.

# BACKGROUND ON YUGOSLAVIA

## Yugoslavia According to the 1981 Census

Total population: 22,424,000

— *The "peoples"*

- Serbs          36.3 percent
- Croats         19.7
- Muslims        8.9
- Slovenes       7.8
- Macedonians    5.9
- Montenegrins   2.5

— *The "minorities" (more than 0.5 percent of the population)*

- Albanians        7.7 percent
- Hungarians       1.8
- Roma (Gypsies)   0.7

— *The "undetermineds"*

- "Yugoslavs"      5.7

Tito's Yugoslavia: The Republics and Autonomous Regions
of Socialist Yugoslavia (1945-1991)

## The Mosaic of Peoples

### Serbs

*Regions:* Serbia, Croatia, Bosnia
*Language:* Serbo-Croatian (Cyrillic alphabet)
*Predominant religion:* Orthodox

### Croats

*Regions:* Croatia, Bosnia, Voivodina (Serbia)
*Language:* Serbo-Croatian (Latin alphabet)
*Predominant religion:* Catholic

### "Muslims" (Islamicized Slavs)

*Regions:* Bosnia
*Language:* Serbo-Croatian (Cyrillic & Latin alphabets)
*Predominant religion:* Islam

### Montenegrins

*Regions:* Montenegro
*Language:* Serbo-Croatian (Cyrillic alphabet)
*Predominant religion:* Orthodox

### Slovenes

*Regions:* Slovenia
*Language:* Slovene (Latin alphabet)
*Predominant religion:* Catholic

### Macedonians

*Regions:* Macedonia
*Language:* Macedonian (Cyrillic alphabet)
*Predominant religion:* Orthodox

### Albanians

*Regions:* Kosovo (Serbia), Macedonia
*Language:* Albanian (Latin alphabet)
*Predominant religion:* Islam

### Hungarians

*Regions:* Voivodina (Serbia)
*Language:* Hungarian (Latin alphabet)
*Predominant religion:* Catholic

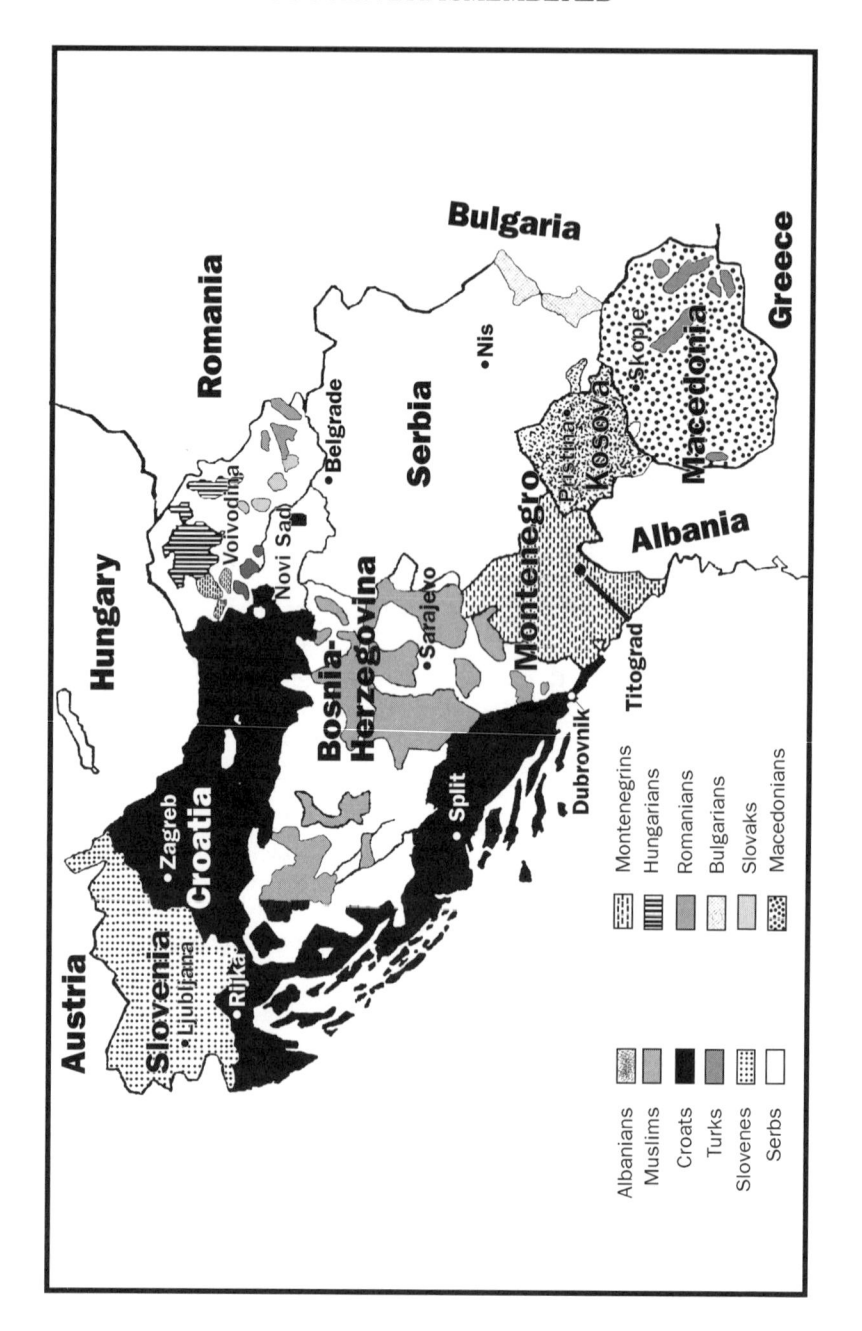

# YUGOSLAVIA DISMEMBERED

## Ethnic Composition of the Republics in 1991*

(Excluding minorities with less than 1 percent of the population)

***Ex-Yugoslavia as a whole:*** Area: 255,804 sq.km. Population: 23,529,000. Percentages: Serbs, 36.2; Croats, 19.6; Muslims, 9.8; Albanians, 9.1; Slovenes, 7.3; Macedonians, 5.6; Yugoslavs, 2.9; Montenegrins, 2.2; Hungarians, 1.4; others, 5.9.

***Bosnia-Herzegovina:*** Area: 51,121 sq.km. Population: 4,365,000. Percentages: Muslims, 43.7; Serbs, 31.4; Croats, 17.3; Yugoslavs, 5.5; others, 2.1.

***Croatia:*** Area: 56,538 sq.km. Population: 4,760,000. Percentages: Croats, 77.9; Serbs, 12.2; Yugoslavs, 2.2; others, 7.7.

***Macedonia:*** Area: 25,713 sq.km. Population: 2,034,000. Perntages: Macedonians, 64.6; Albanians, 21; Turks, 4.8; Roma, 2.7; Serbs, 2.2; others, 4.7.

***Montenegro:*** Area: 13,812 sq.km. Population: 615,000. Percentages: Montenegrins, 68.1; Muslims, 14.6; Serbs, 9.3; Albanians, 6.6; Yugoslavs, 4.2; others, 3.5.

***Serbia:*** Area: 88,668 sq.km. Population: 9,792,000. Percentages: Serbs, 65.8; Albanians, 17.2; Hungarians (mainly in Voivodina), 3.5; Yugoslavs, 3.3; Muslims (in the Sanjak, above Montenegro), 2.4; Roma, 1.4; Croats (mainly in Voivodina), 1.1; others, 5.3.

  ***Kosovo*** *(Kosovo-Metohija, autonomous province within Serbia):*
  Area: 10,900 sq.km. Population: 1,950,000. Percentages: Albanians, 82.2; Serbs, 10; Muslims, 2.9; Roma, 2.2; others, 2.7.

  ***Voivodina*** *(autonomous province within Serbia):*
  Area: 21,800 sq.km. Population: 2,013,000. Percentages: Serbs, 57.3; Hungarians, 16.9; Yugoslavs, 8.4; Croats, 3.7; Slovaks, 3.2; Montenegrins, 2.2; Romanians, 1.9; Roma, 1.2; others, 5.2.

  ***Serbia without Kosovo and Voivodina:***
  Area: 55,968 sq.km. Population: 5,824,000. Percentages: Serbs, 87.3; Muslims, 3; Yugoslavs, 2.5; Albanians, 1.3; Roma, 1.2; others, 4.7.

***Slovenia:*** Area: 20,251 sq.km. Population: 1,963,000. Percentages: Slovenes, 87.6; Croats, 12.7; Serbs, 2.4; Muslims, 1.4; others, 5.9.

* Carried out in the midst of the Yugoslav crisis, the 1991 census was controversial. For example, the Albanians boycotted it; they estimate that they make up nearly 40 percent of the population in Macedonia. See Jean-François Gossiaux, "Recensements et conflits 'ethniques' dans les Balkans," *La Pensée* no. 296, pp. 23-33.

## The Yugoslav Crisis: Names

Abdic, Fikret: Muslim chief executive officer of Agrokomerk conglomerate involved in 1987 financial scandal, in former Yugoslavia member of Communist leadership and federal collective presidency, in 1990 member of Muslim SDA party, then represented SDA in Bosnian collective presidency, in 1993 ousted after declaring autonomous region under his control in Velika Kladusa in Muslim Bihac enclave, in 1994 allied with Serb militias following Bosnian army offensive against his forces

"Arkan": *see* Raznjatovic, Zeljko

Badinter, Robert: French jurist, in 1991 head of commission formed by European Community to advise on recognition of ex-Yugoslav republics

Bakaric, Vladimir: a Croat, Communist leader under Tito

Berisha, Sali: president of Albania

Boban, Mate: former leader of "Croat Democratic Community" (HDZ) in Bosnia-Herzegovina, organizer of Croat militias, "ethnic cleansing," and "republic of Herceg-Bosna" unilaterally declared in Herzegovina in July 1992, ousted in 1994 to make way for Croat-Muslim federation

Cicak, Ivan Zvonimir: jailed for Croat nationalism after 1971 "Croatian Spring," in 1990 founder of Croat Peasants Party (which he has since left), denounced anti-Serb "ethnic cleansing" in Croatia, leader of Helsinki Human Rights Commission of Croatia

Cosic, Dobrica: writer and ex-Communist dissident accused of Serb nationalism under Tito, on June 1, 1992, elected president of rump Yugoslavia, together with Prime Minister Milan Panic challenged Serbian leader Slobodan Milosevic's policies and advocated negotiations to end the war, in June 1993 ousted by Milosevic in alliance with Vojislav Seselj's nationalist Radical Party

Djilas, Milovan: a Montenegrin, Communist leader until Tito, theorized transformation of Communist Parties in power into new exploiting classes, was expelled from League of Yugoslav Communists and convicted in 1954 trial

Draskovic, Vuk: writer, leader of Party of Serb Renewal; first an extreme nationalist, later one of the main leaders of the democratic opposition to Milosevic

Haveric, Tariq: a leader of non-nationalist Liberal Party of Bosnia-Herzegovina, now in Paris

Izetbegovic, Alija: Bosnian Muslim leader, in 1970 author of "Islamic Declaration," for which he was jailed during 1980s, since 1990 leader of Muslim Party of Democratic Action (SDA) and president of Bosnia-Herzegovina

Karadzic, Radovan: leader of nationalist Serb Democratic Party (SDS) in Bosnia-Herzegovina, advocate of "Greater Serbia," organizer of Serb militias and "ethnic cleansing," since 1992 president of the "Serb Republic of Bosnia-Herzegovina"

Kardelj, Edvard: a Slovene, Communist leader under Tito and the regime's main theoretician

Kljujic, Stjepan: Bosnian Croat leader, in spring 1992 ousted by Mate Boban from Croat Democratic Community (HDZ) and Bosnian collective presidency because of opposition to ethnic partition, in March 1994 back in collective presidency of new Croat-Muslim federation as head of new Croat political formation

Kucan, Milan: former leader of reform-minded Slovenian Communists, since 1990 president of Slovenia (first elected over opposition of anti-Communist DEMOS coalition)

Markovic, Ante: a Croat, in 1989-1991 last prime minister of the Yugoslav federation, tried to carry out "shock therapy" to end triple-digit inflation and implement IMF-backed privatizations, came into conflict with governments of republics, founder of Reformist Party (only party to run in all ex-republic elections, later renamed and allied with liberal social democrats)

Mesic, Stipe: a Croat, in 1992 last president of the old Yugoslav federation (imposed by "international community" after Serbs blocked his election), known as defender of Croatian independence, member of ruling Croatian HDZ party leadership, in early 1994 organized split from HDZ in opposition to Tudjman's authoritarian regime and Bosnian policies

Milosevic, Slobodan: since 1986 head of the Serbian League of Communists (in 1990 renamed Socialist Party), since 1987 in effective control of Serbian government, in 1989 elected president of Serbia, reelected in 1992 in race against Milan Panic

Mladic, Ratko: from a Serb family massacred by Ustashes during the Second World War, today a Serb ultranationalist; general in Yugoslav People's Army, commander of army brigades during interventions in Croatian Krajina and Bosnia-Herzegovina, in 1992 when army withdrew from Bosnia stayed behind and became commander in chief of Bosnian Serb "Republic" forces

Nedic, Milan: Serb general in pre-World War II Yugoslavia, during World War II quisling ruler of Serbia under German and Italian occupation

Panic, Milan: Serbian-American businessman, in July 1992 became prime minister of rump Yugoslavia under President Dobrica Cosic, seen at first as pawn of Milosevic, won support among democratic opposition by advocating peace, in December 1992 challenged Milosevic for Serbian presidency and was defeated, then ousted as Yugoslav prime minister

Pavelic, Ante: leader of the Croat fascist Ustashe, head of the so-called Independent Croat State set up in 1941 under German and Italian domination (which included Bosnia-Herzegovina) and organizer of "ethnic cleansing" against Jews, Serbs, and Roma (Gypsies)

Rankovic, Aleksandr: Serb, Communist leader and minister of interior under Tito, carried out severe repression against Kosovo Albanians until his expulsion from League of Yugoslav Communists in 1966: suspect of fomenting a centralist plot, he opposed decentralizing reforms then being introduced

Raznjatovic, Zeljko (pseudonym "Arkan"): worked for secret police under the old regime, now organizer of Serb militias and "ethnic cleansing" in Bosnia-Herzegovina, under protection of Milosevic government until 1994; his election as deputy from Kosovo after suppression of the province's autonomy in 1990 was seen as a real provocation, and he was not reelected in December 1993 elections

Rugovo, Ibrahim: writer, leader of Kosovo Democratic League, leader of nonviolent Albanian resistance, clandestinely elected president of their unilaterally-declared Kosovo Republic

Seselj, Vojislav: leader of Serb nationalist Radical Party, originally united with Vuk Draskovic and other advocates of Greater Serbia, split with Draskovic in order to ally with Serbian President Milosevic (while Draskovic stayed in opposition and gave up Greater Serbian positions), from late 1993 criticized Milosevic openly as Milosevic evolved "peace" policy and began denouncing crimes committed by Seselj's militias in Croatia and Bosnia-Herzegovina

Silajdzic, Haris: prime minister of Croat-Muslim federation, associated with more secular wing of President Alija Izetbegovic's Muslim SDA (Party of Democratic Action)

Starcevic, Ante: under Austro-Hungarian rule, leader of extreme right nationalist, very anti-Serb Party of Right, later considered by fascist Ustashes as their forerunner

Susak, Gojko: Croat extreme rightist, Herzegovina native, returned from exile in Canada, Croatian defense minister under Tudjman, gave military support to Mate Boban's policies in "Republic of Herceg-Bosna"

Tito, Josip Broz: main Communist leader since 1937, during World War II led Partisan resistance forces, president of Yugoslavia from 1945 until his death in 1980

Trumbic, Ante: Croat leader, after World War I headed "Yugoslav Committee" representing Serbs, Croats, and Slovenes of former Austro-Hungarian empire in negotiations with Serbia over forming a common South Slav state

Tudjman, Franjo: Croat former Partisan, ex-Communist and historian, charged with Croat nationalism and persecuted under Tito, leader of anticommunist, nationalist HDZ (Croat Democratic Community) coalition that won Croatia's first free elections, president of Croatia since it became independent

## Yugoslavia in Historical Context: Key Dates

(See also the complete chronological appendix at the back of the book)

### Independent Balkan Kingdoms

**800-1400**  Medieval kingdoms form: Bosnia, Croatia, Serbia, Bulgaria.
**1000-1100**  Great Christian schism: Croats and Slovenes become Roman Catholic. Serbs, Montenegrins, and Macedonians become Eastern Orthodox. Bosnia acquires its own, "heretical" church.

### Ottoman and Austro-Hungarian Rule

**1300-1700**  Slovenia, Croatia, and Voivodina become part of Austria-Hungary. Ottomans conquer Macedonia, Serbia, Albania, and Bosnia. Montenegro remains independent. Serb warriors settle Austrian-ruled Croatian border area (Krajina). Many Bosnians become Muslim.
**1830**  Serbia becomes autonomous within Ottoman empire.
**1878**  Serbia wins independence from Ottomans. Austria-Hungary occupies Bosnia-Herzegovina.

### The Three Yugoslavias

**1918-1941**  "First Yugoslavia" (centralized under Serb domination).
**1941-1945**  World War II: Pro-nazi Ustashe rule Greater Croatia (including Bosnia). Ustashe carry out "ethnic cleansing" against Serbs, Roma (Gypsies), and Jews. Communist-led Partisan resistance creates postwar Yugoslavia. Serb nationalist Chetniks fight both fascists and Partisans.
**1945-1991**  "Second Yugoslavia" (Tito: federal, nonaligned, under single-party rule).
**1991-**  Slovenia, Croatia, Bosnia, and Macedonia declare independence. Serb nationalists rule "Third Yugoslavia" (Serbia plus Montenegro). Violent conflicts in Croatia, Bosnia, and Macedonia.

# Introduction

# The Yugoslav Crisis: An Overview

When Yugoslavia was founded in 1918,[1] its people found themselves for the first time in a common state.[2]

For the defenders of "Yugoslavism," these peoples had enough of a "community of fate" to come together, whatever the differences among them that they might have inherited from the past. For opponents of the common Yugoslav state, on the other hand, the differences (religious, cultural, even linguistic) between communities were and have remained too great for the creation of a single "nation." This is why Yugoslavia was, according to them, an artificial country.

I read in all the newspapers, Yugoslav or foreign, that Yugoslavia was a fiction. Then I am a fiction too—I'm the same age as this Yugoslavia—and I don't exist.[3]

Rada Ivekovic belongs to a new minority, whose members suffer from no longer being able to be Yugoslav—worse, being unable even to call themselves Yugoslav. "In my eyes," she says, "this word 'Yugoslav' (just like 'Serb' or 'Croat') has been compromised." It has been compromised by all those who wanted a Yugoslavia for the sake of their own power, imposed by force; and by those who want to affirm their own identity by denying others *their* identity. But is the plurality of identities, histories, cultures *the cause* of Yugoslavia's failure and current fragmentation? Is it in fact the cause of the war?

Some people think so. They parade their contempt for those they call "nostalgic" for the Yugoslav past. In their eyes the present is by definition an advance over the past. They see the break-up of the federation as a profound movement of emancipation. For them, the declarations of independence have simultaneously put an end to the Communist yoke and to a Yugoslavism that was essentially oppressive. Xavier Gautier characterizes this kind of assertion quite well under the title, "History: Wholesale Lies and Falsifications":

> It has become fashionable at cocktail parties—from July 1991 on in Germany, from October 1991 on in France—to uphold this "revealed truth," that Yugoslavs never wanted to live together and Serbs always wanted to see Croats die. They've been killing each other ever since, so the proof is there for all to see! The authorities in Zagreb have backed this credo in every possible way. According to this new rehash of official history, eight turbulent nations, forced by an "iron hand" to share the same space for seventy years, finally demanded to separate from one another.[4]

From this viewpoint, the current break-up of the old Yugoslavia into nation-states should be seen not as a step backwards, but as an advance toward models that were "achieved" earlier elsewhere in Europe. According to historian Dimitri Nicolaidis, "Basically, the Serbs and Croats are headed in the right direction." After all, what do they want? "Far from wanting to go backwards, they are trying to look more like us (Western Europeans)." The author thinks that a nation-state demands "a homogeneous society, without which no political community and no sovereignty is possible."[5] Serbo-Croatian policies should remind us, the historian suggests, of the 1923 Treaty of Lausanne between Greece and Turkey, sponsored by the League of Nations, which made mandatory an exchange of populations (affecting one third of the Greek population). Or they should remind us of the "repatriation" of Germans from Eastern and Southeastern Europe, sanctioned by the Allies in 1945.

Building "homogeneous" nation-states necessarily requires that each people affirm its *difference* from the others (in this case, from the other Yugoslav peoples). History and its myths go to show "the long-term impossibility of living together"; and History also offers the "proof" that this or that territory "belongs," or should belong, to this or that nation. The languages that resemble each other most closely are "cleansed" of one another: in the self-proclaimed "Serb Republic" in Bosnia, local speech is being purged of "non-Serb" expressions. In Croatia, a new dictionary of differences between Serb and Croat lays down the list of words whose use is now obligatory and the words that can cost you your job. Croatian newspapers are full of Old Croat expressions that the population doesn't understand. The works of one of the greatest Croatian writers, Miroslav Krleza, has just been "translated" into "Croat" from its original language (Serbo-Croatian) for the new textbooks.[6]

In fact, Croats, Serbs, and Bosnians all basically speak the same language, Serbo-Croatian.[7] Aside from the different alphabets—Cyrillic and Roman—dialects survive that in reality are more regional than ethnic. The three Bosnian communities speak the same dialect; Croats who live in the Serbian province of Voivodina speak the same way as the local Serbs; and similarly, Serbs in Zagreb can hardly be distinguished from Croats in the republic's center. On the other hand, the people on (Croatia's) Dalmatian coast speak differently. In any event, long experience has resulted in exchanges between dialects, each major dialect incorporating words taken from another's lexicon.

According to most linguists the differences were smaller than those between British and American English. Nonetheless, some people think that these are not dialects of a single language, but separate languages: this is in fact a *political* choice.

Those who think this way consider that the crisis of the Yugoslav state and the war have the same causes: the need to put an end to a state that is artificial *because it is heterogeneous.* "Citizenship" and "nationality" must be made to coincide.

The distinction between "citizenship" and "nationality" is difficult to understand in countries where the two are the same, where people make no distinction between saying they are "French citizens" and saying they are "of French nationality." But actually there are two types of nation-state:

— The French ("Jacobin" or "republican") type of nation is political: it consists of a community of persons who live and work on the same land and have the same rights and duties.

— The German or Zionist type bases the nation on an ethnic-cultural community.

In Eastern European countries, in the Yugoslav federation as in the USSR, there was a distinction between *citizenship* (affiliation with a state) and *nationality* (in the ethnic and cultural sense). These were thus multinational countries.[8]

The logic of "ethnic cleansing," aimed at bringing all the Serbs together in a single country, comes closer to the German type of nation. According to this conception of an "ethnic nation," Turks who were born, lived, and worked in Germany could not (until changes that were made recently) be full German citizens, even if they spoke the language and had lived and worked in Germany for a long time. People of German origin living in the ex-USSR are by contrast automatically German citizens, even if they lost contact with Germany and forgot German long ago. The law of return in effect in Israel works the same way. This same "model" has been put to work in Croatia, where a Croat emigré becomes a citizen while thousands of Serbs who have lived and worked in Croatia do not.[9]

The Yugoslav example (and not only the Yugoslav example) shows that there is a right-wing, racist way of defending the right to be different: the dominant nation's "purity" must be "protected" by excluding the others. No "nation of citizens" is immune to this tendency—consider the United States, with its "English-only" and other anti-immigrant campaigns. The search for "homogeneity" becomes a means of exclusion whenever jobs are hard to find.

This is a painful logic for all those who identified with Yugoslavia. Some of them "felt" Yugoslav because they came from mixed families; others because they valued a diverse cultural "space" based on citizenship without denying anyone his or her ethnic origin, or because they were reacting against exclusionary nationalisms. It is difficult to measure these people with a statistic. Individuals were free to claim whatever nationality they wanted, within the limits of official nomenclature; so national identities were evolving. But it is very significant that more than 1.2 million "Yugoslavs" declined to state an ethnic identification in the 1981 census.[10]

It must be emphasized that people's choice of nationality did not have the same implications in the past, when the census had no personal consequences, as it does now, when people are choosing "their country" or even "their side." It makes a difference when your job, your property, your safety and even your survival, and your children's as well, depend on your making the "right choice."

The need to make such a choice is particularly fraught for those who felt that they were "Bosnians" first and Serbs, Croats, or Muslims second.[11] They were generally attached to Yugoslavia as well.

So faced with retrograde nationalisms and with the retreat toward building exclusionary, ethnically based nation-states, some people look back appreciatively to the Yugoslav past.

The Yugoslav past? For some this means the first Yugoslavia, between the world wars, seen as a Jacobin state in which citizenship and nationality were joined together. For others it means Tito's

Yugoslavia, in which the one citizenship was combined with recognition of different nations and nationalities (minorities) in a system of ethnically mixed republics. For still others it means the project that was taking shape behind the liberal, antinationalist orientation of the last Yugoslav government, the government of Croat Ante Markovic, who turned in 1989 toward privatizations and a European market without frontiers.

Together with the advocates of "Yugoslavism," we reject the thesis that living together was impossible. This pseudo-interpretation of the crisis only *conceals the existence of other options* (since narrowed down). It legitimates chauvinist, exclusionary nationalist policies in both Serbia and Croatia. Today it justifies the dismemberment of Bosnia-Herzegovina: if the Yugoslav blend was artificial, the same must be true of the Bosnian blend.

But *national questions are real questions about democracy*, and there is a distinction between national aspirations and nationalism as an exclusionary ideology. Uncritical celebration of any particular period of the Yugoslav past does not help us understand why the first Yugoslavia failed, Titoism went into crisis, and Ante Markovic's policies faced powerful resistance.

In short, the "Yugoslav project" is in crisis, and the crisis has to be explained. It has repercussions for the Bosnian crisis, which was initially the result of outside aggression but not *only* the result of outside aggression.

Any new project for reunion, any alternative to the retreat to nation-states, has to go by way of criticism of the past and recognition of the right to separation. But how can this right be applied to communities split among several countries and intermingled with other communities? How to make this right compatible with the right to a multiple identity or the right to stay together? The "Bosnian question" poses the right to self-determination not just in the old form, but also in a new form for those who felt they were "Bosnian," claiming an identity based on mixing and tolerance. These Bosnians are not represented and thus not heard in the negotiations, which only recognize "pure" identities.

In the current period of economic crisis and "globalization," when integration becomes more difficult even as massive migrations occur, each type of nation-state runs up against its limits. There is no universal "model" that has proved itself and established a revealed truth. There were different histories, in which capitalism emerged differently and appropriated spaces and workforces differently.

The fragility of the most thoroughgoing "republican" model of citizenship can be seen for example in the United States, where any immigrant can become a citizen and any citizen is theoretically the equal of any other. Even this stronghold of egalitarian ideology has, in periods of economic or social crisis, been shaken by gusts of exclusivism. In the 1840s and 1850s it was Irish and German Catholic immigrants whom the "Know-Nothing" party considered unworthy of equal citizenship. In the 1920s it was Eastern and Southern Europeans whose immigration was restricted on grounds of racial inferiority. In the 1990s it is the turn of Asians and Latin Americans to bear the brunt of anti-immigrant prejudice. Ironically, those citizens who preach exclusion are all themselves descended from immigrants; while the descendants of North America's original inhabitants, and of African slaves brought to work southern plantations before the Puritans first immigrated to New England, share least of all in the benefits of equal citizenship.

In reality the most solid phases of nation-state-building (when citizens who are socially, sexually, and culturally very diverse develop a subjective bond to a nation) depend on neither an impossible homogeneity nor a particular ("correct") ideological approach. They depend on fairly specific historical contexts, which cannot be reproduced in any and all circumstances, whatever the virtues of a particular model of citizenship.

The American "melting pot," which as we have noted is neither as egalitarian nor as melted as is sometimes claimed, basically "worked" thanks to the political and economic power of attraction of a very great power. This is basically why most U.S. citizens are proud above all of being "American," whatever their cultural bonds with the countries they came from.

The French Revolution was also an exceptionally good mold for unifying a territory that had been linguistically, religiously, and socially very divided. After "France" emerged from a long, turbulent history, it was a combination of fierce repression of particularisms (children were forbidden for a long time to speak any language besides French at school), social compromises, military victories, and finally advantages linked to socioeconomic growth that consolidated the French "republican model." Democracy was organically linked to economic growth, which made it possible to tolerate conflicts and keep them from exploding.

We will therefore analyze Yugoslav national questions as well in their evolving socioeconomic and political context. It was "worth it" to be Yugoslav (or Swiss, Belgian, Czechoslovak, or Canadian) as long as people "got something from it" (rights to their own identity and socioeconomic security). *Rightly or wrongly, in times of crisis, separation and identification with a smaller community can seem a route to more security and higher status.* How many Ukrainians (or say Slovenes) favored separation from a crisis-ridden USSR (or say Yugoslavia) simply because they hoped that their country would do better economically?

Since socioeconomic and historical contexts explain the strengths and weaknesses of existing "models", there is no one-way "historic trend" that must triumph everywhere. True, the "disappearance of all the federations built in the years 1918-22 on the debris of empires" is a fact,[12] but were they all only "post-imperial makeshifts," to use Joseph Krulic's expression? And is their disappearance only a result of the crisis of the so-called socialist countries?[13] Trends in the opposite direction also exist, in the East as well as in the West. At the same time that the Russian Federation is fragmenting, the newly independent states are re-creating links, or retaining the old links. The trend toward creating a multinational Europe does not evoke the "nostalgia for the old empires."

So we lean toward one side in this discussion: toward rejecting pseudomodels that claim to be universal, and rejecting an ethnic fatalism that would also imply a historical fatalism. Atrocities in the war are giving aid and comfort to the ruling idea that the communities could not and did not want to live together. Those who start from this conviction are led to belittle the importance of all those who are now trying to resist separation, or who are suffering from it. As for the past, it can only be painted black, without shades of gray: the crisis "proves" that there was nothing good in it.

Even those who admit that there were several decades of relative tranquillity insist that it was only "a manufactured calm in the context of a regime whose methods were Stalinist."[14] Besides, "the relaxation of the regime's pressure led automatically to the revival of conflicts between nations." In other words, according to this kind of approach, nothing was gained in the past. No progress had been made that would allow us to attribute the periods of "calm" to anything but repression. And the crisis is ultimately the expression of interethnic conflicts that were previously stifled. Thus Bernard Féron answers the question, "Why was Yugoslavia able to survive until the last decade of the century?" by saying that "it held more or less together for about thirty years thanks to two factors: the dictator Tito's historic weight" and the role of the international "environment."[15]

We agree of course with the idea that the lack of democracy was at the root of Titoism's crisis. We will return to this, and to the international factors that did play an important role in the Titoist regime's mode of legitimation. But should this lead us to dismiss the contributions of the Yugoslav past? That would be using the crisis as an excuse to ignore the whole richness of Yugoslavia's history and everything we can learn from it.[16] It would be deliberately blinding ourselves, over and above the risk of deafening ourselves to the arguments of those who still want to live together and to find new forms of union.

We will thus evoke the Yugoslav peoples' *past* as well as their present, without any pretention of writing history (other works have this function), taking care to read and listen to different versions of the same history[17] and to draw on some of their lessons. But in analyzing the past—its periods of stability as well as its darkest days—and in analyzing the present crisis, we will stress the *interaction* of national, economic, and political issues.

In this regard we are critical of "nationalist" interpretations of national issues and of Yugoslav setbacks. We show that it is not any more "natural" to build a Serb or Croat ethnic state than to build a Yugoslav or Bosnian state. The periods of Yugoslavia's or Bosnia-Herzegovina's greatest cohesion corresponded to the times when the populations concerned experienced real gains in living standards and rights. It was by contrast *threats to these gains during the 1980s*—not interethnic hatred—that gave rise to Yugoslavia's fragmentation. The socioeconomic and political crisis of the 1980s was in this respect a turning point.

We think that the worldwide and Yugoslav promarket offensive during those same 1980s, far from offering an alternative to the country's break-up, was a key factor in its disintegration. Nationalism in this context served several different purposes, because the various kinds of authoritarian governments sometimes had conflicting economic logics. There are thus several wars within the war, connected to genuinely difficult problems of self-determination.

The crisis was not just a crisis of so-called Communist regimes, but a result of the *clash and interaction of two crises.* Contrary to the dominant illusions at the end of the 1980s, the Europe of the Maastricht Treaty is not a (socioeconomic and political) "model" that can be counterposed to the nationalist disintegration of Eastern Europe. The same contradictory tendencies (between "globalization" and the reaffirmation of nation-states) are at work in the West as in the East. The same questions (What individual and collective freedoms? What kind of democracy, in the service of what way of managing resources?) are unresolved in both regions. The same orientations toward racist exclusion and closing of ethnic frontiers are being propagated in defense of steadily scarcer jobs.

*Chapter 1* focuses on the theme of "evolving national identities." We show that it is no more "natural" to be a Serb, Croat, or Muslim than to be Yugoslav, and that so-called interethnic conflicts have to do with political choices. Political choices have divided each community, making no distinction between "Balkan" (savage?) peoples and "European" (nonviolent, civilized?) ones.

*Chapter 2* sketches a critical portrait of the Titoist regime. First it "borrows" Serb, Croat, and Slovene nationalist spectacles in turn in order to perceive this regime's different traits, piecing together the elements of truth that each nationalism enables us to see. Then we try to see Titoism steadily and whole.

*Chapter 3* analyzes "the wars within the war." The effects of free market ideology in the 1980s exacerbated the overall crisis of "Titoism." By way of Yugoslavia's fragmentation, we take up the issue of the preconditions for self-determination. We defend the thesis that the blame for this war must be shared, though unevenly.

*Chapter 4* illustrates our problematic by making use of the Bosnian symbol, taking off from an ethnic, socioeconomic, and political analysis of this "miniature Yugoslavia" (as Bosnia-Herzegovina is often called today).

In *Chapter 5* we discuss the responsibility of the "international community" for the Yugoslav conflict. Despite their different spheres of influence and diplomatic interests, the Western powers have shared an approach based on pragmatic, evolving—and disastrous—*realpolitik.*

The *Conclusion* makes clear that the stakes in the Yugoslav crisis are important not only for the peoples of ex-Yugoslavia, but for Europe and the future of the world.

The war has inflicted wounds since it began. Some of the wounds will not heal. Wasn't this the war's real aim: to propagate hatred? But still none of the republics, whether self-declared or not, is homogeneous, in spite of 2.5 million people displaced in Bosnia—3.5 million refugees from the entire Yugoslav area, on top of 750,000 people who have applied for asylum abroad.[18] The situation continues to change quickly. War could still break out again in Croatia, or in Kosovo, and in that case in Macedonia as well, setting the Balkans on fire.

People must open their eyes. A stable peace can only be founded on a set of consistent criteria, on equal treatment for the different communities, and on allowing ethnic mixing rather than ruling it out. But what kind of protections are needed? What new political, cultural, and socioeconomic links? What rights must citizens, peoples, states, and supranational organisms have? Can anyone still pretend today that the Europe of the Maastricht Treaty, which was still fatally attractive to Eastern Europe at the turn of the decade, answers all these questions? Can anyone still pretend that the virus of nationalist racism comes only out of the East?

# 1
# Indeterminate Nationalities

## "NATURAL" NATION-STATES?

Those who think that every people (meaning every ethnic group) has the "natural" destiny of building "its country" run into problems very quickly, particularly in the Balkans. How is the country's territory decided? How is the people itself defined? These are actually historical constructions.

### *The logic of ownership*

Historians are virtually at war today over the distant past in which the first, medieval Slav states were born and died. They are all trying to legitimate "their" countries' territorial demands against their rivals. But the same stretches of land can be covered with several layers of history.

The great powers have exploited ethnic differences through the centuries in order to divide and rule. As early as the sixteenth century, for example, Austria granted the Serb peasants in the Austro-Hungarian empire's Krajina border region a special status as warriors in order to ensure the empire's defense against Turkish pressures. This is why, even though the land they lived on was Croatian "territory" under Hungarian rule, they were not subject to joint Croatian-Hungarian rule but attached directly to Austria. Croatia's rejection of this "foreign body" on its territory is one dimension of the anti-Serb Greater Croatia policy. The historical dimension is reinforced by social and cultural dimensions. The Croatian government is easily moved to contempt for these Serb peasants of the poor Knin region. These peasants "by tradition" are easily moved to express their political resistance through guerilla warfare.

This helps explain why the Croatian Serbs do not see themselves as a "minority" in a Croat country, and do not want to be one. The only historic period in which they were a "minority" under direct Croat rule was the time of genocide carried out against Serbs, Jews, and Roma (Gypsies) by the Ustashe-ruled Independent Croat State during World War II. Nor do they accept being treated as "occupiers" of "Croat" territory, since they have lived there for centuries. Nonetheless, if we go still further back in time, the Knin Krajina where there is now a Serb majority was the cradle of the medieval Croatian kingdom—just as Kosovo, with an Albanian majority today, was the cradle of the medieval Serbian empire!

Yet nationalist logic means that in setting up "our" country, historical criteria can be used here, ethnic criteria can be used there, and strategic criteria can be used somewhere else. And adversaries can be denied the "rights" that "we" demand for ourselves.

The Kosovo Albanians[1] do not want to be treated as a minority either, still less as occupiers. Serb historians often reiterate that Kosovo was the cradle of the first Serbian empire, and the site of the great battle lost to the Turks in 1389. But "the Serbian empire of the Middle Ages was no more a nineteenth or twentieth century-style nation-state than other medieval kingdoms were," Joseph Krulic reminds us. The emperor reigned over a population composed of diverse peoples. "Albanian-Serb relations were good precisely because the nation-state had not been invented. A good part of those fighting on the Serbian side at the battle of Kosovo were Albanians, though Serbian politicians today rarely mention this."[2] Since then there have been centuries of migrations, and Kosovo has become an Albanian-majority area, undergoing the hazards of war and territorial rearrangements among the great powers.

According to Albanian historians, if we go still farther back in time, millenia ago, Kosovo is where the Albanians' Illyrian ancestors established their community. As Michel Roux emphasizes, both sides' interpretations often have "the same underlying conception of history. Each of the two peoples declares the temporal priority and legitimacy of its presence in Kosovo in order to assert ownership."[3]

But apart from history, there is the *reality* of populations that speak different languages and do not mix. There is an overwhelming Albanian majority in the province (more than 80 percent), reinforced by a very high birth rate in Albanian families (seven or eight children per family on average as against two in Serb families).[4]

Michel Roux asks, "Does anyone have the right, based on this or that period of the past, to make themselves exclusive 'owners' of a territory?"[5]

## *Evolving peoples*

But is the "people" itself, the nation, the ethnic group, better "defined"?[6]

In the Greater Croatia of 1941, Catholics *and Muslims* (Islamicized Bosnian Slaves) were considered Croats. We will examine the Muslim case later. But the definitions are also being slanted on the Dalmatian coast, which was long ruled by Venice and resisted both the Austro-Hungarian and Ottoman empires. Dalmatia was also, to a greater extent than central Croatia, a center of the Titoist partisans' antifascist resistance. Oriented toward tourism and the outside world, it has a mixed identity today that is different from central Croatia's. Regional political groupings, not Tudjman's ruling party, are in the majority. People on this Adriatic coast tend to call themselves "Dalmatians" or "Istrians" rather than Croats, above all when they want to resist a too-centralist government. We have already stressed the weakness of any linguistic definition of "Croatness."

Are definitions any clearer on the "Serb" side?

Serb nationalism is rooted in a tradition of confrontation and warrior epics, notably the much-touted battle of Kosovo. Resistance to foreign rule, made larger than life in songs, poems, and literature,[7] have nourished both a strong national pride and a tragic "revanchism," an urge to national self-assertion in the aftermath of perceived national humiliation. Refusing to convert to the oppressor's religion[8] played an essential role in the affirmation of a distinct identity. Serbs have also kept the Cyrillic alphabet. A religious approach would emphasize Orthodoxy as the distinctive sign of Serb identity. But not all Orthodox are Serbs (any more than all Catholics are Croats); and over time religion has lost ground on all sides. (Will it make up lost ground now?) The "Greater Serbian" nationalist approach traditionally emphasizes the common language instead. (But are all European Francophones "French," even in Belgium and Switzerland?)

The notion of "Serbness" has in fact been widened or narrowed over the years in light of political factors. In the nineteenth century, when Croat and Serb intellectuals hoped for a coming together of South Slav peoples, they worked on unifying the grammar of what they saw as two dialects of a single language. Today on the contrary, in a period of crisis, people are working to create two languages, Serb and Croat, as far apart from one another as possible. Even a "Bosnian" language is making its appearance.

Today plans for a Greater Serbia generally remain within the framework inherited from Titoism: they aim to bring together those who considered themselves Serbs in Tito's Yugoslavia. But "Serbhood" is expandable for those who consider that the Macedonian, Muslim, and Montenegrin peoples "don't exist," or are "Tito's artificial creations." Those who share this last viewpoint nonetheless have to deal with a historic, subjective heritage and a political choice, crystallized among populations that themselves do claim to be distinct peoples.

If Serbs, Croats, and Slovenes did at least have some sort of identity that was recognized when the "Kingdom of Serbs, Croats, and Slovenes" was formed, we will see that their status as "nations" was nonetheless not guaranteed. The other Yugoslav communities were recognized as "nations" only under Tito.

The part of historic Macedonia[9] acquired by the first Yugoslav state was called, significantly, "South Serbia." Bulgaria always denied the existence of a Macedonian nation, while Greece still considers itself the legitimate heir of historic Macedonia.[10]

To take the ethnic group closest to the Serbs, are the Montenegrins Serbs? They speak the same language: the Serb dialect, written with the Cyrillic alphabet. The majority of Montenegrins are Orthodox. But if you ask them, some of them will say they are Serbs, while others (whose numbers may be increasing today for political reasons) will say they are Montenegrins. And the Montenegrin identity has arisen from *history*. At first the embryo of an independent state called Zeta during the eleventh century, Montenegro was part of medieval Serbia, then came under Venetian and later Turkish rule. But it secured its autonomy as early as the sixteenth century and its independence at the end of the seventeenth, though it was recognized as a state only in 1878.

This independence, conquered and protected early, forged the specific identity of the Montenegrin mountaindwellers, even though a (variable) part of this people identifies as Serbs. The Serbs gladly "claim" the Montenegrins by "scientifically" denying the absence of sufficient criteria to define a separate Montenegrin nation.[11]

The articulation of religion with ethnic identity was common in the Balkans. Given that the great religious divides of the past (Catholicism versus Orthodoxy and Islam versus Christianity) have traversed the Yugoslav space from end to end,[12] they have contributed to carving out different *national identities.*

The "mini-Yugoslavia" called Bosnia-Herzegovina bears all the marks of these differentiations. Born in the twelfth century, Bosnia-Herzegovina became in the fourteenth century one of the strongest of the independent South Slav states. It had its own Bosnian church, sometimes connected to the Bogomil heretics.[13] With the coming of Ottoman rule in the fifteenth century, the conversion of a certain number of Bosnian Slavs to Islam[14] was undoubtedly in part a *defense against Catholic and Orthodox persecution.* Conversion also allowed the (Catholic, Orthodox, or Christian heretic) Bosnian Slavs who chose to become Muslims to avoid taxes paid by "infidels" and to take part in local government.

Whether they were Islamicized (often identified and identifying as "Turks"), Catholic or Orthodox, the Slavs of Bosnia-Herzegovina spoke the same language, even though the little-used Arabic alphabet was introduced to write it and a regional Bosnian speech existed. But *language is not enough to unify a people* (nor even necessary: Swiss people for example speak four different languages). A political and socioeconomic cement is also needed. The strengths and weaknesses of Bosnia—or Yugoslavia—have to be analyzed in each historic period in relation to this basic precondition.

Life in Bosnia, punctuated by major migrations, did not consist only of harmony and tolerance. Literature bears witness to this, as in Yugoslav Nobel Prize-winner Ivo Andric's story "Letter from 1920."[15] It is true that religious affiliation cut across social and cultural differentiations. Mixed marriages remained rare as long as religious influences were still strong and the country as a whole was backward. The antifeudal peasant uprisings of 1875-1878 were directed both against the Bosnian oligarchy and against the Ottoman government that relied on it.[16] The majority of the Orthodox (Serbs) were serfs under Ottoman rule. The majority of landowners were Islamicized Slavs who later settled in large numbers in cities (and became secularized).

Both the strength and weakness of the Ottoman empire consisted in the fact that it tolerated different religions while linking religion with political and social hierarchies. Bosnia is often described in completely opposite terms: either ideal tolerance through the centuries, or age-old divisions and hatreds. *The two aspects have gone together,* and evolved through time with the country's industrialization in the twentieth century.

Tolerance (which compared favorably with Queen Isabella's religious persecutions in fifteenth century Spain[17]) allowed diverse religious communities to be welcomed and respected. The communities were able to form their own leaderships through their ecclesiastical hierarchies. The churches were responsible for education and justice (some with more resources than others, obviously) through religiously based community institutions (millets).[18] As Xavier Bougarel shows in his fine analysis,[19] communities lived side by side for centuries without mixing (mixed marriages were real communal and personal melodramas). There was no common citizenship in the Ottoman empire, since social status varied widely according to religion. But there was a "neighborliness" (komsiluk) accompanied by rituals (for neighbors' drinking coffee together, for instance) and appearances at each others' festivals. Customs remained different, without borrowing and reciprocal influences being excluded.

This tolerance for differences made coexistence possible, and was the empire's strong point. But it also *perpetuated and crystallized differences.* Social and political differentiation, even oppression, brought conflicts and even lasting hatreds in their wake, and were liable to break out into open warfare. They broke out into class struggles (landlord-peasant conflicts) or political struggles, in historical contexts of imperial crisis and nation-state-building wars.

On the level of ethnic identity and national loyalty, Bosnian (and Yugoslav) history thus bore a heavy weight of inevitable conflicts—but also sources and periods of rapprochement:

During the centuries of Ottoman rule, the Islamicized Bosnian Slavs called themselves "Turks" (or "Ottomans"), *identifying with the source of their security and status*: a great power in whose social hierarchy they were, as Muslims, an integral part. The crisis of Ottoman rule and Bosnia's coming under Austro-Hungarian (Catholic) rule opened for Muslims a long period of uncertain identity. They lost their link with Turkey (and their investment in it, since it was no longer an advantage), without being able (or wanting) to identify with other Slav peoples (Croats and Serbs, who both tried to win Muslims over and at the same time rejected them as "opportunists" or traitors to the Serb cause). In censuses Muslims largely called themselves "undetermined."

The independence won by Serbia and the prestige of its nineteenth-century fight for freedom were very attractive for Bosnian Orthodox peasants, who revolted against their Muslim landlords. They naturally identified with the Serbian kingdom, which strengthened the link between ethnic and religious definition in this period. It was the same for Bosnian Croats, who took advantage of neighboring Croatia's political autonomy by going to schools in Zagreb.

At the same time, other factors counteracted narrow ethnic and national differentiation. Bosnians in general felt an attachment to their "native ground," the ethnically mixed region where they lived, the local speech, their real ties with their neighbors. In addition, there was modernization, the declining influence of religion, urbanization (meaning new apartment buildings and neighborhoods that were no longer ethnically distinct, unlike people's old home towns), migrations, and the enlargement of common space due to industrialization. Building Yugoslavia was part of this process of leaving behind narrow local spaces. But not everyone benefitted in the same way. The processes of mixing, expanding social horizons, and upward mobility hurt or passed by some areas and social categories.

Today in Bosnia-Herzegovina there is still a conflict between city and countryside which leaves a definite mark on all the communities—all the extreme nationalists have their main social base in the countryside—but reflects a peasant majority among Serbs and an urban majority among Muslims. It is also the case that, with the coming and going of different foreign rulers and the rise of different nation-state projects, the different churches came to support different political logics.

Serb and Croat nationalism have both denied (for several decades now) the distinctive reality of the Muslim community; they have both found "historic evidence" justifying their territorial claims on Bosnia-Herzegovina. Serb nationalism has staked its claim in a directly aggressive way, thirsting for revenge on the "Turks" and their "allies." These Serb nationalists consider the Muslims to be "historic traitors," to use Nenad Fiser's expression:[20] Serbs who have betrayed their own people.

Croat history does not fit this model, since the Croats were sometimes adversaries and sometimes uneasy allies of the Hungarian or Austro-Hungarian governments. They shared the religion of their Catholic oppressors. Their conflicts with these rulers did not take the form of frontal opposition, as the Serbs' more often did; instead they tried to make deals with their foreign rulers and to win some autonomy, much as the Muslims did with the Ottomans. The Croats sought in some periods to win the Muslims over to the cause of building a Croat state. They hoped to integrate Bosnia into Croatia, as actually took place in the Ustashe's Greater Croatia. From that standpoint the Muslims were "'flowers in the Croat garden'—which the flowers are unlikely to take as a reassuring compliment from the gardener," as Nenad Fiser remarks.[21]

The consolidation of the republic of Bosnia-Herzegovina and the national recognition of the Muslims in Tito's Yugoslavia could only reinforce the Muslims' determination not to be turned into Croats. That made them into traitors to the Croat cause as well as the Serb cause, so that an inevitable symmetry grew up between the ultimate hostility of Serb and Croat nationalisms toward the Bosnian Muslims. In Zagreb as in Belgrade nationalist propaganda labels Muslims automatically as "fundamentalists" in order to provide a cover for territorial ambitions. On both sides the "Muslim nation" is dismissed as "Tito's creation."

Tito did have a pragmatic attitude toward national questions, particularly in Bosnia. He managed to recognize real differences, while at the same time he sought to play the rival territorial claims of Croat and Serb nationalism against one another in order to consolidate his power and Yugoslavia's frontiers. He also tried in his nonalignment policy to be evenhanded in his treatment of the Muslim community as compared with the Serbs (Orthodox) and Croats (Catholics).

All the communities developed their different identities in the course of major historical changes by choosing what they saw as "preferable" for their political interest or identity. We have seen that the independence won by Serbia during the nineteenth century was attractive for Bosnia's Orthodox inhabitants. But the ideas of the French revolution and the possibility of building a Yugoslav state after the fall of the Ottoman and Austro-Hungarian empires encouraged many Croat and Serb intellectuals to go beyond a religious definition of the nation to a broader, linguistic approach (all those who speak Serbo-Croatian make up one single people). Even the linguistic approach was too narrow: the idea of a "nation of citizens" spread with the integration into Yugoslavia of peoples speaking other languages (in particular Macedonian—officially recognized under Tito—and

Slovene, not to speak of non-Slavic languages such as Hungarian and Albanian). It coexisted in any event with persistent ethnic identities. There was a similar phenomenon in Bosnia.

With the passage of time and the advance of industrialization, the Muslims were secularized and became less and less religious (though their victimization in the war and their isolation may be reversing this trend now). Many of them called themselves "Yugoslav" in national censuses. Mixed marriages (about 40 percent of all marriages in Bosnia's cities) encouraged this development. A substantial proportion of Muslims reacted to the break-up of Bosnia by calling themselves "Bosnians" rather than Muslims, much as a certain number of Bosnian Serbs and Croats did. So the break-up of Yugoslavia has provoked *simultaneously*: nationalist polarizations toward Serbia and Croatia; in reaction to the war, a Bosnian Muslim identity that is equally exclusive;[22] and the contrary identity of those who are fighting to affirm a people of Bosnian citizens or a multinational Bosnia made up of several peoples like the old Yugoslavia.

Thus a Bosnian "national identity" also has to be recognized.[23]

People who champion the most inclusive Yugoslav approach are often dismissive of these special identities, which they see as "provincial," as a kind of backward-looking particularism. Today they see themselves as champions of the transcendence of the nation-state. But there is more than one way to transcend the nation-state. The logic of overarching Yugoslavism is not necessarily more generous than the logic of narrower nation-states. The exclusive nationalism of small nation-states can be echoed by a nationalism *on another scale*, which can be just as intolerant.

Is there for example only one single Slav or Yugoslav ethnic group? Is any nation within it—the Serb nation or the Croat nation—"artificial" by definition?

## THE EXPERIENCE OF THE FIRST YUGOSLAVIA

Building a common country does not require a past free of conflicts. What it requires is substantial reasons to overcome past conflicts. Neither does joining together require a preexisting homogeneity; it only requires sufficient political will and a real social and economic basis for a better life.

There is no single Yugoslav "project." There have in any event been several different Yugoslavias, and other forms of union have been (and still are?) possible. In other words a setback does not necessarily "prove" that the attempt was "artificial." The real question is therefore how to understand the causes of past setbacks and conflicts: not by means of the "biological, apolitical and irrational" explanations (as Stanko Cerovic calls them[24]) given by nationalists, but in a historical way, including all the cultural, political, and socioeconomic dimensions of history.

### *The Serb dynasty's unitary state*

The project of bringing together the South Slavs fulfilled aspirations that were first embodied in the "Illyrian movement" of Slovenes, Croats and Serbs in the nineteenth-century Austrian empire. Encouraged when the "Illyrian provinces" of Slovenia and Dalmatia were united from 1809 to 1814 under Napoleon's rule, the movement found literary expression in the 1850 Vienna agreement between Croat and Serb writers. Opposing Ante Starcevic's Party of Right, which demanded a Croat national state, the Yugoslav-oriented Croat-Serb coalition won a majority in the Zagreb Diet and kept it from 1906 to 1918.

The Croats' desire to resist Magyarization (assimilation into Hungary) and the Slovenes' desire to resist Germanization (assimilation into German-speaking Austria) were encouraged by the Serbs' struggles for emancipation from Ottoman rule and the formation of an independent Serbian state. With the collapse of the Austro-Hungarian and Ottoman empires, and thanks to the redistribution of influence among the great powers at the end of World War I, forming a common country suddenly became a real possibility.

The post-World War I Yugoslav union would be experienced and envisaged in several different ways. Sometimes it was seen as uniting three different parts of *one single nation* (Serbs, Croats, and Slovenes were called "one people with three names"). From this standpoint cultural, religious, and historrical differences were seen as secondary relative to what bound the nation together. But the union could also be seen as finally making possible the national affirmation of distinct communities that had previously been oppressed. This second possibility could even have taken the form of a long-term project for a federal or confederal, i.e., multiethnic state. But for political currents whose ultimate goal was the creation of a nation-state for each ethnic group, such a union could only be temporary: a stepping stone toward separation.

The key to a viable Yugoslavia had to be found and built on the level of the political and socioeconomic system. The union would have meaning and long-term prospects only if the new country's citizens and communities, individually and collectively, could live better in it than before.

The first Yugoslavia was born as the "Kingdom of Serbs, Croats, and Slovenes." But in fact the three peoples were not equal in it.

During the nineteenth century, equipped with an army and an independent state that they put at the service of the common cause of South Slav emancipation, the Serbs came to see themselves as the saviors and framework of a single South Slav nation. "Victory over Bulgaria reinforced further Serbia's confidence in its power and its conviction that it is the natural center toward which all the others must gravitate: that it is the representative and guide of the entire nation."[25] This is why Serb nationalists said in 1918 that they were "disappointed" by the other peoples' "ingratitude." The Serbs had "given up their country" for the other peoples when they could have expanded it, they said, since they were among the war's "victors."

The majority of Slovenes were Catholic; they had been ruled for centuries by Austria. But they were proudly and jealously protective of their language, which they had never stopped speaking despite strong German pressure. This Slav tribe had never had its own country during the Middle Ages; even its name was a nineteenth century invention. Like the Croats, the Slovenes used the Latin alphabet. But unlike the Croats, they did not try to obtain a kind of territorial autonomy and governmental role in the Austro-Hungarian empire. The first Slovenian state thus emerged from Tito's Yugoslavia. The paradox is that Yugoslavia's least "nationalist" nation was the first and even the best positioned to win its independence. In earlier times, Slovenes' relationship to the Serb dynasty of the first Yugoslav state was less conflicted than the Croats'.

Like the Serbs, but unlike the Slovenes, the Croats had their first monarch and medieval state during the ninth century. The country fell quickly under the sway of the Hungarian dynasty, and remained under Hungarian or Austro-Hungarian rule until the First World War. But even under Hungarian rule the Croats won a measure of autonomy, embodied by the end of the thirteenth century in a Diet—the

*Sabor*—and in a Croatian *Ban* (Duke). The desire for a federal state was thus very strong among Croats, even among those who were pro-Yugoslav. The first Yugoslavia's unitary structure would radicalize the Croat currents that were most in favor of independence.

The first negotiations with the Serbian government were carried on by representatives of South Slavs of the Austrian empire united in a "Yugoslav Committee" of political refugees, presided over by the Croat Ante Trumbic. The two parties to the 1917 Corfu declaration declared "that Serbs, Croats, and Slovenes are one people and must form one monarchical state under the Karageorgevic dynasty."[26] Negotiations resumed after Austria's defeat, this time between Serbian representatives and a "National Council of Serbs, Croats, and Slovenes" of the Austro-Hungarian empire. This National Council advocated a project different from the Corfu declaration's: a confederation between Serbia and a Serb-Croat-Slovene state of Austrian Slavs. This idea was rejected by the Serbian prince regent.

The Italian threat accelerated the formation of a common country, which also included the Voivodina, Montenegro, and Bosnia-Herzegovina. Unresolved institutional discussions about the final form of the new state were referred to a constituent assembly. But the confederalist and federalist proposals were defeated. As a result the Croat deputies decided to boycott the new country's parliament. The Communist Party's deputies did the same: the Communist Party and Comintern denounced the kingdom as a "prison of peoples" and tool of the great powers. The Communist Party and its activities were banned.

This first Yugoslavia had no republics, only administrative divisions. In 1929 the "Kingdom of Serbs, Croats, and Slovenes" took the name Yugoslavia, and was transformed into a Serb royal dictatorship. The dictatorship imposed a kind of centralist or "unitary" Jacobinism. All national communities and minorities suffered from this policy. But the Serbs identified more than others with this Yugoslav state, which had united Serbs who had been living under several alien governments and was "their country" to begin with, since it rested on an army created in their struggle and on a Serb dynasty.

Political crisis followed political crisis in the context of a chronic economic invalidism exacerbated by the worldwide depression. Yugoslavia remained a "normal" country of the capitalist periphery in which a "market economy" reigned. Dependence on foreign capital went together with underdevelopment: pervasive backwardness of entire regions, particularly those that had been under Ottoman rule; a largely agricultural economy with impoverishment on a massive scale; and export-oriented production. The international stagnation of the interwar years had severe repercussions on the country's fragile economy.

The first Yugoslavia was an overall failure. But as Joseph Krulic stresses, "the ghost of the centralized French model haunted Yugoslavia in 1929-1933."[27] The Slovene judgment of the period cited by Bernard Féron is different: "[W]e were suddenly thrown out of the European framework we had lived in into an Asiatic framework."[28] People slide all too quickly (today as in the past) toward a distinction that borders on racism, gladly taken up by Slovenes and Croats, between Yugoslavia's "Asiatic" (or "Balkan") peoples on the one hand—those in the "South," formerly under Ottoman rule—and the "Europeans" on the other; between the civilized Catholics and—the others. The writer Predrag Matvejevic complains:

> Every day we run up against people who claim to uphold "national" causes that are in fact merely regionalist causes; "Europeans" who are still grasping nationalists; "citizens of the world" who put their religious, ethnic, or racial affiliation above any principle or any other value....[29]

The first Yugoslavia's failure does not prove the impossibility of living together. But it does raise real issues: on the one hand the counterproductive nature of an authoritarian, Jacobin model after centuries of differentiation among different communities, without a real popular mobilization for a common goal; on the other hand the inability of an externally-oriented "market economy" to bring about a new balance between Yugoslavia's rich and poor areas.

Domination by the Habsburg and Ottoman empires had interrupted the development of the South Slav medieval kingdoms. It is true that those who were relatively more lucky—those who came under Austro-Hungarian rather than Ottoman rule—enjoyed some beginnings of industrialization. The first Yugoslav state did not mesh well with these more developed regions, a fact that worsened its dictatorial character. Quickly taking fright at peasant uprisings and workers' strikes, the government was also very dependent on foreign capital, which did not help with the development of the poorer regions. National, regional, and social (particularly peasant) problems conspired to undermine the first Yugoslavia's legitimacy. It broke apart as soon as the Axis armies invaded in 1941.

## WOUNDS OF WORLD WAR II: INTERETHNIC CONFLICTS?

The occupation resulted in the Axis forces' cutting up Yugoslav territory into several different states. All the quisling regimes were marked of course by the domination of Nazi Germany and fascist Italy, which supported governments in their image or in their pocket. The Albanians, like the Croats, had the misfortune of "enjoying" an independent state under fascist rule during the war.

One might have expected the antifascist struggle to be carried on on "national" bases which would later be the foundations for separate countries, freed from the foreign oppressor. This turned out not to be the case. It is doubtful whether the different communities *could* have effectively resisted German and Italian political and economic domination if they had had at the same time to cut themselves apart from one another in order to build separate countries. *This was one of the key raisons d'être of the second Yugoslav union.*

The atrocities in the fratricidal struggles during World War II were still no less gruesome than the atrocities of the war being fought in ex-Yugoslavia today.

There were the atrocities of Greater Croatia, which swallowed up Bosnia-Herzegovina. We said earlier how "Croatness" was defined: Catholics and Muslims were "Croats." The others—Jews, Roma, Serbs—had to disappear. Thus the "ethnic cleansing" perpetrated by the Croat Ustashe[30] and Muslim fascist commandos against Serbs, Roma, and Jews, with a level of violence that disquieted even the Nazi regime. This violence had a government at its disposal. And it was carried out by the "European" part of Yugoslavia—a region just as civilized as Germany.

But there was also the revenge taken by the "Chetniks."[31] They answered the Croat and Muslim fascists' genocide with their own ethnic massacres of Croats and Muslims—although this violence was not always implementing a policy supervised by the Chetnik high command. Whole national communities were collectively found guilty and treated as enemies. The whole Croat people was found guilty of (Ustashe leader) Ante Pavelic's fascist policies. Islamicized Slavs were found guilty of first "becoming Turks," then "allying with the Ustashe": they had betrayed the "Serb cause" twice. This is the ideology that is still to be found today in the Serb militias carrying out "ethnic cleansing" in Bosnia.

The 1941-1945 war in Yugoslavia, simultaneously a world war, a civil war with interethnic massacres, and a war of national and social liberation, caused more than a million deaths in a Yugoslav population that totalled about 16 million. The extermination of the Jewish and Gypsy peoples, victims of the Nazis, of the Serbian quisling Nedic, and of the Ustashe rulers, was almost total. Hundreds of thousands of Serbs were killed, and proportionally at least as many Muslims.

The most violent conflicts and massacres were concentrated in Bosnia-Herzegovina. So was the strongest resistance, aided by a topography conducive to guerilla warfare. The Communist-led Partisans set up their high command in Jajce, near Sarajevo. There they decided to create a second, federal Yugoslavia. The Yugoslav federation was foreshadowed in the way armed struggle was organized and by the countergovernment that was forged in armed struggle, embodied in 1943 in the underground parliament called AVNOJ (after its Serbo-Croatian initials). The future republics and provinces were formed in the armed struggle, at the same time as the Communist Party.

Some Yugoslavs chose to support fascist policies. Others—Serbs, Croats, Slovenes, Albanians, Muslims, Jews, etc.—resisted them actively, together, in a fight against other currents among their own peoples. The armed struggle organized by the Partisans, led by the Yugoslav Communist Party, made this possible. The Partisans made a multiethnic antifascist resistance possible because they had a Yugoslav federalist project, which was counterposed *both* to any idea of resurrecting a "unitary" Yugoslavia or its social and national policies *and* to any idea of building "ethnically pure" nation-states imposed by fascist means. The Partisans made a multiethnic antifascist resistance possible because they stood *both* for recognition of differences *and* for unity. This is why they won.

In other words: the 1941-1945 war included both battles and rapprochements between communities. So the conflicts cannot be interpreted as proof of eternal hatred or of the impossibility of living together. The interethnic massacres during World War II were the expression of particular *political orientations*—just as the *unity* of different communities against fascism during the same war was the expression of a *different* political orientation.

But this does not in itself explain *how* people can live together.

### Tito's Yugoslavia: "prison of peoples" or "minority dictatorship"?

The paradox of Tito's Yugoslavia is that, viewed through two different nationalist lenses, it can be judged in two different ways. We will try them both on in the next chapter. But we will not take at face value the official historiography of a regime that never tolerated pluralism. Neither will we take at face value the caricatures produced by some of the Tito regime's opponents.

A precondition for mutual trust is complete openness about all the dark pages of the past—including of course the Stalinist practices of the Yugoslav Communist Party.[32] But to conceal the importance of the Partisan-organized resistance in the name of anti-Stalinism, or ignore the positive effects of Yugoslav Communism's partial break with Stalinism, would be to echo the ideological manipulations of history committed by the former governments that called themselves Communist. It would cloud our appreciation of the importance of the historic turning point constituted by Slobodan Milosevic's reorientation in 1986—and his alliance with some of the currents that lay claim to the Chetnik heritage.[33]

# 2

# Titoism's Balance Sheet

> **Tito's Yugoslavia: Key Dates**
>
> **1948**  Yugoslav-Soviet split.
>
> **1950**  Law on workers' self-management adopted.
>
> **1955**  Khrushchev visits Yugoslavia and apologizes publicly.
>
> **1956**  Nonaligned Movement meets in Yugoslavia.
>
> **1965**  Reform decentralizes economy and extends role of market.
>
> **1968**  Student movement and strikes suppressed.
>
> **1971-1972**  Croat nationalist movement ("Croatian Spring") repressed.
>
> **1974**  New constitution gives veto right to each republic and province.
>
> **1980**  Tito dies. $20 billion debt revealed. Decade of crisis begins.

## NATIONALISTS LOOK BACK AT TITOISM

By the end of the 1980s, Tito's Yugoslavia was seen in Belgrade as an irreversible failure, and as "anti-Serb" besides.[1] In the Slovenian capital Ljubljana, Yugoslavia was seen as an unbearable economic burden. In Zagreb, Croatian President Tudjman denounced "Yugoslavism" as "by its very essence anti-Croat."[2]

## Through Serb lenses

As for Serbia, it was included among the rich Yugoslav republics that had to contribute to the Federal Development Fund, even though its per capita income remained slightly below the Yugoslav average. The economic crisis inspired a "nationalist" reading of its consequences: that they were the result of "anti-Serb" prejudice.

> The anti-Serb coalition revealed itself more openly and with less political tact than ever before in the matter of the rate of contribution to the Federal Fund.... The attitude toward Serbia's economic disadvantages shows that the politics of anti-Serb revenge has not weakened with the passage of time. On the contrary, pushed onwards by its own success, it has grown steadily stronger, ending ultimately in genocide. The discrimination against Serbia's citizens who, because of the equal representation of the republics, have fewer positions in the federal administration and fewer delegates in the Federal Assembly than the others, is politically indefensible....[3]

The explanation of this "anti-Serb" policy was found in the line of the Communist International, which denounced the first Yugoslavia (dominated by the Serb dynasty) as a "prison of peoples"; in the composition of the Communist Party's historic leadership (Tito and Bakaric were Croats, Kardelj a Slovene); and finally in Tito's line, which was said to be summed up in the slogan: "A weak Serbia means a strong Yugoslavia." The "creation" of provinces (Voivodina and Kosovo) within Serbia alone, and the equal representation and right of veto granted the provinces as well as republics under the 1974 constitution, were interpreted as "anti-Serb" discrimination. Scattering the Serbs in several different republics, subjecting them to a "dictatorship of anti-Serb minorities," ensuring political underrepresentation of the Serb majority (since there was parity): it all led to "anti-Serb genocide," particularly in Kosovo and the poorest, Serb areas of Croatia.

In reality, "Titoism" as a system of government sought simultaneously to divide and rule and to unite and rule. It did not "artificially" divide Yugoslavia into republics and "create" new nations: Kosovo, Voivodina, and the various republics corresponded to real historic regions and had a place in the multinational whole. Even if the Serbs were not gathered together in Serbia, the same was true for the Albanians, Croats, and Muslims in relation to "their" republics.

True, Serbia was strictly speaking only one of eight parts of the federation in the 1970s (including the two provinces that became quasi-republics). But if Serbian sovereignty ended at the gates of Kosovo and Voivodina, the Serbs as a people shared sovereignty with the other peoples in Croatia and Bosnia. Nor was that artificial, since ethnic mixtures were the result of vast historic migrations and economic development, not of administrative manipulations. By trying to deny the reality of Kosovo in order to return to a mythic, medieval state of affairs, the Serbian government itself pushed Kosovo away from Serbia. As for the economic grievances, what they described was not anti-Serb policies but real tensions between the rich republics (Croatia and Slovenia, with higher-than-average living standards) and the less developed republics.

### Through Croat lenses

As long as the "center" was in Belgrade, it was easy to suspect it of being "pro-Serb." So the same regime that was called anti-Serb in the capital was labelled "pro-Serb" (even pro-Greater Serbia) by Croat nationalists.

Tensions between the most developed republics and the others were expressed in disagreements among economists from the 1960s on: over planning versus the "socialist market," as well as over the optimal growth rate for the richer regions.[4] Those who advocated greater decentralization of resources and easing of redistributive mechanisms argued that the country as a whole would grow more quickly if the most developed republics were allowed to develop more quickly. The growth would "naturally" spill over to the other regions, they said.

True, the economists who argued most forcefully in these debates for redistributive mechanisms and who were most critical of the market were undoubtedly Serbs. But these Serbs expressed the viewpoint of the less developed regions in general. They did not begin from a "Serb" standpoint, but from a classically Marxist approach. While some economists played an important role in the introduction of the "socialist market" in 1965, social and national tensions weighed heavily in the background of the reforms. These tensions would get worse, notably in the 1971 "Croatian Spring."[5]

As soon as wages depended less and less on the *work* done, and more and more on *sales* in the market, pressures grew from regions with a good position on the world market (Slovenia and Croatia in this case, but the phenomenon is widespread) for more economic autonomy. Croatia had obvious natural advantages for tourism. Even if the hotels on the Adriatic coast received their food supplies from Voivodina in Serbia, they were the sellers of the "finished product," tourism, and they received the hard currency for it. The Croat nationalist movement's demands that Croatia should keep these currency earnings (despite the supplies provided by other republics upstream from the hotels in the division of labor) doubtless contributed significantly to a strong centrifugal dynamic.

As early as 1971 Croatian economists put forward statistics "proving" how much Croatia was "exploited" by the "Serb" center. (Today, for Istria and the Dalmatian coast, the oppressive "center" that is stealing away their hard currency is—Zagreb!) The fact that the Yugoslav capital and its federal institutions were actually located in Belgrade encouraged this interpretation. Even though the gap between rich regions and less developed regions was growing, the rich felt that they would be even richer if not for the transfers required by the central government. On top of these economic grievances came statistics on Serb overrepresentation in the government and army apparatus: 60 percent of the Yugoslav army's officers were Serbs. This ethnic unbalance in the country's administration and police grew worse after the suppression of the Croat nationalist movement in 1971.

But was this movement suppressed because it was *Croat*? Or was it suppressed in the same way that any opposition to the regime's line of the moment was suppressed, regardless of nationality?

In fact those who criticized the Stalinist purges before 1948 were suppressed; the "Cominformists" who wanted ties with Moscow after the 1948 Tito-Stalin split were suppressed; the Albanian uprisings in the same period were suppressed (under the orders of the Serb minister Aleksandr Rankovic—the same man who was "pushed aside" in the 1960s when he opposed the new decentralizing policies). The leaders of the Serbian student movement, who criticized the market reforms in 1968, were put in jail; then the liberal leaders of the Croatian Spring who wanted *more* market reforms were put in jail; and soon afterwards, for good measure, Serbian advocates of more market reforms were put in jail. Then in the 1970s and 1980s the Kosovo Albanians, who had been demanding their own republic since 1968, had another turn at suffering repression.

In short, the repression in Croatia increased Serb overrepresentation in the apparatuses *for political reasons, not ethnic reasons.* Similarly, while the majority of army officers were Serbs, this was not because of deliberate ethnic discrimination but because of a *long historical, socioeconomic, and political heritage*: the Serbs' long warrior past, and their disproportionate participation in the antifascist struggle in Croatia and Bosnia-Herzegovina because they were victims of genocide there. Finally, the army and administration were not attractive for many Croats; while by contrast for many Serb peasants, particularly in poor areas of Croatia, becoming an army officer was a big step forward in life and an occasion for village celebrations. Were there not centuries-old traditions behind this?

As for the Croatian Spring's economic demands, they were essentially *granted by the arbiter Tito* in the 1974 constitution (more "anti-Serb" politicies, said the nationalists in Belgrade!). This combination was typical of Titoism: suppression of any independent movement, combined with concessions from above. True, the concessions were more often economic than political.

The regime also seemed very much afraid of anything that would be reminiscent of the Ustashe nationalist demons in the field of language policy. For example, Croat intellectuals signed a petition in 1968 protesting against an administrative codification of Serbo-Croatian. There were clearly genuine frustrations around this subject, since repression made no distinction between nationalism directed against others (such as we are unfortunately seeing on the rise today in the policy of "ethnic cleansing" of the Croatian language) and the hope for freedom of expression in all the language's dialects.

Repression helped to fuel extremism (and create future "post-Communist" heroes) instead of containing it. Croats came to feel that they had to bear the burden forever of the Ustashe past; Serbs came to feel that they had to pay forever for their domination of the first Yugoslavia.

### *The Slovene view: "Europe" against "the Balkans"*

From the beginning of the 1980s on, Yugoslavia had a foreign debt of about $20 billion, declining production, and a worsening balance of trade, along with hyperinflation that reached almost 1,500 percent in 1989. After a decade of crisis that affected the whole of the ex-federation, Slovenia, the richest republic, had a per capita Social

Product[6] *more than twice the Yugoslav average and seven times as high as Kosovo's* (the Serbian province with an Albanian majority).[7]

"Better last in the city than first in the village": that was the state of mind often expressed in Slovenia. "The city" was "Europe"; the village was Yugoslavia. Hope of joining the winners' European Union more quickly than the other republics was encouraged by ties with Germany, which had become Slovenia's main trading partner and foreign investor. West Germany's share of Slovenian exports rose from 15 percent in 1985 to 22 percent in 1990, and West Germany's share of imports rose from 20 to 23 percent, while the USSR's share fell to 13 percent of exports and 6 percent of imports. Out of $430 million in foreign capital invested in Slovenia in 1990, $165 million came from West Germany and $104 million from Austria—and many of the Austrian investments came from West German companies' Austrian subsidiaries.[8]

Tensions grew up between the republican governments and the Belgrade central government over management of the foreign debt. Republics' refusal to apply the austerity plan adopted by the government became more determined when the Serbian government began to print more and more money for purposes of its own. Republics were not in a hurry to pay their shares into the federal treasury while it was being used to finance an army that was increasingly seen as a threat.[9]

While the gap in per capita income kept widening to Slovenia's advantage and to a lesser extent to Croatia's, these two republics' economists and spokespeople continued to complain about their "exploitation." True, the transfer of resources allocated to the Development Fund was not negligible: 1.94 percent of the Social Product of all public firms was diverted to the fund. During the 1980s the fund made on average 17 percent of investments in eligible areas (nearly 52 percent of investments in Kosovo—something that the Serb interpretation of "discrimination" fails to take note of).

The rich republics in turn had advantages that they failed to take into account. Slovenia finished and then exported products received from other republics at favorable prices. Besides, almost 60 percent of Slovenia's external sales went to the Yugoslav market as late as 1991. But Slovene nationalists made do with figures that minimized the republics' interdependence.[10] Instead of taking a critical look at the socioeconomic mechanisms at work and the bureaucratic management of the aid, nationalists were content to emphasize the "burden of aid" to the "incompetent" communities of the Yugoslav South. They praised the Slovenes' and Croats' "European, civilized, efficient" (Catholic) traditions as opposed to the "Balkan" peoples' traditions—a form of flattery than won a certain audience in Western Europe.

Behind the racist dimension of this discourse was a dismissal of the mutual benefits of federation for the different republics and of the system's advantages for the developed republics. Slovene nationalists also underestimated the difficulties in trying to compete at world prices in a capitalist market in crisis.[11]

True, once it was a separate country Slovenia might be in danger of finding itself subordinated to its powerful German neighbor. Slovenia's independence and national identity might be at risk. But Slovenians have to go through the experience. Slovenes' affirmation of their identity intensified sharply in any case when the Yugoslav army intervened in June 1991, which served the cause of Slovenian independence well. After the Yugoslav army's rapid retreat from Slovenia in summer 1991, the widening of the war in Croatia and then in Bosnia-Herzegovina hastened the decline of the former Yugoslav market and reinforced Slovenian separatist aspirations. Even in the framework of a reestablishment of relations with Slovenia's former Yugoslav partners, no kind of unitary state could be imposed again.[12] This was already the inescapable reality of the 1980s.

## WAS THE SECOND YUGOSLAVIA ARTIFICIAL?

The failure of the first Yugoslavia did not necessarily mean the end of any Yugoslav project. Some say today that the second Yugoslavia like the first was "artificial," imposed by a dictatorship which this time around was dominated by the Communist Party. Were the Communists able, after fighting the first Yugoslavia as a "prison of peoples," to impose this new Yugoslavia against its peoples' will?

The absurdity of this hypothesis seems all the more flagrant when we remember that on the eve of the Second World War the CPY had barely 5,000 members.[13]

If Communist rule had been based simply on repression, if the CP had not won a legitimacy shown in the mushrooming of its membership during the war, the new government could not have survived several decades without major explosions, given the deep wounds that the war left behind. Those wounds constituted major reasons for the peoples to no longer share a country. The break-up of Yugoslavia in 1940 could have given a head start to alternative, anti-Yugoslav projects.

The new Yugoslavia that emerged from the war was based on a critique of the previous attempt. It was deeply marked by the circumstances of its birth: it was the product *both* of genuine popular uprisings that legitimated Communist leadership and brought about victory, *and* of domination by the CP, which was structured on the basis of the different republics but still a single party. The Tito-Stalin conflict and the break with the Soviet Union in 1948[14] had long-term ambiguous effects. But this ambiguity, made up of partial breaks and reforms within a Stalinist model, was part of the regime's particular mode of legitimation and its particular way of maintaining its one-party rule.

What would the boundaries and institutions of the new country be? Until the 1948 break with Stalin, the perspective of a Balkan Union (and perhaps even a Danubian Union) remained open. Tito had proposed specifically that Albania and Bulgaria join the other republics—contrary to Stalin's proposal for a federation of two states, one Yugoslav and one Bulgarian, which he thought he could control more easily.[15] The cold war, the Tito-Stalin break, and the tensions between the Yugoslav and Albanian CPs signed these projects' death sentence.

The break with Stalin in 1948 and the abandonment of the Balkan project resulted in fierce repression of the Kosovo Albanians,[16] the only ones to rise up against the new regime. The status of autonomous province granted Kosovo within the Serbian republic was a compromise: keeping Kosovo within Serbia responded to Serbs' deep psychological attachment to an area that symbolized their past. On the other hand, autonomy was meant to acknowledge the existence of an Albanian majority and past on that same land. The content of autonomy would depend on the evolution of the regime within Serbia itself.

## CONTRADICTORY ASPECTS OF TITOISM

A constant factor in "Titoism" was *combining repression and concessions*: granting from above part of what had been demanded from below, after having suppressed any independent movement and any chance for real political pluralism. This explains why the system, far from being frozen in immobility, evolved in major ways. It responded through successive reforms to the tensions and imbalances that arose at each stage.

### An evolving pragmatism on national questions

The Communist leaders formed a multiethnic, pragmatic leadership on national questions. Concerned above all with consolidating power, they knew that any Yugoslav state dominated by one particular nationality would be doomed to fall apart, just as any Yugoslav state that denied all national differences would be doomed to fall apart. Titoism meant bureaucratic stifling of nationalisms that were seen as dangerous (Croat, Serb, and, particularly until the 1970s, Albanian), but not of national identities in general. As Rastko Mocnik makes clear, Titoism even fostered the expression of Slovene, Macedonian, Muslim, and (from the 1970s on) Albanian national identities.[17]

The single Yugoslav *citizenship* had been distinguished from the beginning from the different *nationalities,* which were the basis for collective, cultural, religious, and political rights (there were several official languages, and schools, publishing systems, and universities for each official tongue) within the federative system.

The national communities that were recognized as "peoples" or "nations" (*narod* in the ethnic sense) were each granted a republic of their own whose borders corresponded more or less to historic regions. But no national community was joined together as a whole in a single region, for historical reasons. In other words, the republics' frontiers were not ethnic frontiers. Tito's Yugoslavia consisted of six republics. It recognized six constituent "peoples" or "nations" (Serbs, Croats, Slovenes, Macedonians, Montenegrins, and, from 1961 on, Muslims).

The expression "national minority" was seen as degrading, or associated with ideas of second class citizenship and threatened status. In its place the term "nationality" was introduced (*narodnost* as opposed to *narod*—the distinction is difficult to translate). "Nationalities" were communities who already had a country of their own outside Yugoslavia, like the Hungarians (15 percent of the population in Voivodina) or the Albanian majority in Kosovo. The Roma or Gypsies were a special case as an ethnic community, since they had no country anywhere.

The "national minorities," whether they were called *narodnost* like the Hungarians or Albanians or not, were not considered as "constituent" peoples of Yugoslavia: they had not deliberately taken part in forming the federation. Therefore they did not have the right to secede: only the "nations" that were supposed to function on the basis of consensus had the right to self-determination. The national reality and consciousness of the peoples who were called *narodnost* was quite varied and obviously evolving, depending on their rights and experiences. Hungarians never demanded a change in their status. The Kosovo Albanians began to demand the status of republic in 1968, at a time when their rights were increasing.

In the early days of the Titoist regime the republics were subordinated to the federal center in several ways: the hypercentralism of the party that dominated the state; appointment of officials from above; centralized planning. From the 1960s on, the relationship began to be reversed. The republics' (and provinces') congresses became more important, and new officials from their dominant ethnic groups rose within their state apparatuses. Like Yugoslavia, Albania denounced the Soviet intervention in Czechoslovakia in 1968. In the wake of this convergence there was a thaw in Yugoslav-Albanian relations, accompanied by an increase in rights and economic aid for the Kosovo Albanians (investments financed mainly from the Development Fund; Albanian-language schools and a university in Pristina; development of cultural relations between Kosovo and Albania).[18]

The Yugoslav system took on hallmarks of a confederation with the 1974 constitution. The collective presidency had to respect the "ethnic key," and its chairperson was drawn from a different nationality each year. There was equal representation (and a right of veto) for each republic regardless of size as well as for the provinces of Kosovo and Voivodina—which gave the provinces a veto weapon against the Serbian government and the status of virtual republics. All this was denounced by Serb nationalists during the 1980s as a "minority dictatorship," "excessive rights," and above all an "infringement on Serbian sovereignty over Serbian land." The demand for a Kosovo republic was rejected as a prelude to secession. Acquiring the status of a "nation" (people) with a republic of its own did in fact mean acquiring the right to self-determination.

## A conflicted economic decentralization

The Communist leaders knew that the system's overall stability depended on its capacity to overcome the first Yugoslavia's failures in two ways: to overcome the country's underdevelopment and supply people's basic needs; and to reduce regional inequalities. This implied a redistributive logic that was very centralist at the beginning, but later succumbed to pressure from the rich republics.

There was also the issue of Yugoslavia's relationship to the world market. Until the end of the 1970s there were in fact different "modes of regulation."[19] The single-party political system managed the relationship to the world market by combining market mechanisms with new kinds of planning in varying proportions, which left sometimes more, sometimes less decisionmaking power to the republics and the self-management bodies. It mixed centralism in some areas and decentralization in others with a greater or lesser degree of openness to the outside.

Self-management was powerless in face of either the bureaucratic plan or the market. We can conclude from this that self-management needed a different kind of regulator—democracy—in order to realize its potential for progress. In reality, the system's lack of openness, and the lack of control over strategic, macroeconomic choices and results by those most affected—in short, the lack of political democracy—undermined any kind of solidarity. Market relations only made this impenetrability and fragmentation worse. The bureaucracy was as parasitic on the market as it had been on the plan.

The repression of social, political, and national movements that were seen as subversive went together with a parallel extension of self-management and national rights during the successive reforms through the late 1970s. These factors would in turn generate new tensions and yet more reforms, introduced in a very bureaucratic way, which would lead to the system's ultimate failure.

Nevertheless, the second Yugoslavia's first three decades were a time of development and constantly rising living standards for all its republics and provinces.

The most prosperous period was the time of combined planning, market, and self-management (from 1952 until the 1965 reform, which abolished planning). This is what the Croatian economist Branko Horvat says about it:

Between 1952 and 1966, Yugoslavia's lag behind France's development fell from 130 years to 53; behind Belgium's, from 100 years to 43; behind Sweden's, from 90 years to 44; behind Italy's, from 50 years to 10....

Some have claimed that this success was due less to workers' management than to the scale of foreign economic aid. This is false. Economic aid amounted to about 100 million current dollars, i.e. roughly equivalent to the output of a single firm. Total economic aid for the whole period from 1951 to 1992 was, in constant dollars, less than the value of funds sent home by emigrant workers during 1981 alone; and yet after ... 1981, the economy stagnated.[20]

In other words, the main causes of success as well as the main causes of crises have to be found within the changing system itself.

## THE REALITY OF THE 1980s CRISIS

Throughout its four decades, Tito's Yugoslavia experienced many conflicts. But they were not "explosive" conflicts. They could be defused by the combination of repression and concessions mentioned above. Comparisons with the limited living standards and rights in neighboring countries, or with the prevailing conditions in the first Yugoslavia, worked out in the end to the regime's advantage—enough to its advantage, at least, for the system to be maintained while it was transformed.

Confederalization and economic decentralization enabled the single-party regime to put off a looming crisis. They created "shock absorbers," which allowed the system to tolerate scattered strikes and a certain degree of cultural and ideological pluralism—as long as this did not lead to any organized challenge to the regime.

But there was not a good enough "regulatory system" to let the economic actors set consistent criteria, ensure economic equilibrium, and fix binding overall objectives. The lack of political democracy interfered with any real, pluralist evaluation of the different systems that were implemented at different stages. It hindered any attempt to measure the advantages and side-effects of the different reforms or to set common priorities. The big decisions were taken "elsewhere" in a way that few could see or understand. The price to pay for a system of decentralized rights without overall democracy turned out to be a general spirit of "looking out for number one."

The 1970s was the last decade of growth. But the growth went together with a growing debt, which was suddenly made public at the beginning of the 1980s. This debt of about $20 billion began as a consequence of the system's growing inefficiency. But it was also the result of an uncontrolled entry into the world market. Foreign loans had been plentiful during the 1970s, when petrodollars were being recycled toward the South and East. The debt became a tool used by the International Monetary Fund (IMF) to intervene practically, materially and politically in Yugoslavia's internal affairs. There were people inside the country who were willing to do the IMF's bidding.

The debt in fact marked the beginning of the end for the system, in a context in which socialist ideas (which had supposedly been applied in Yugoslavia) were going into crisis. The moral and political crisis of a bureaucratized Communist party, ravaged by corruption[21] and the rise of nationalism, only grew worse as repression intensified in the 1970s. Austerity policies had to be imposed on resisting self-management organs. Strikes spread in successive waves during the 1980s. Meanwhile the central government's policies came into conflict with the republican governments: the federal authorities were actually paralyzed throughout the 1980s.

The increase in the republics' rights and powers, combined with the crisis of communitarian values, led to a reinforcement of nationalism as a basis of the republican governments' legitimacy, for which their own working classes paid the price. Strikes were most common in the most industrialized republics, Slovenia, and Croatia. Workers streamed out of the League of Yugoslav Communists (the renamed Communist Party), which for a long time had valued their membership. In 1989 the workers of a Croatian industrial center with a very mixed population came to Belgrade and called for a general strike. Their town was called Vukovar.[22]

After years of growth, the three pillars of the system—living standards, social rights, and national rights—collapsed during the 1980s. "Yugoslav self-managing socialism" could no longer keep its promises. The crisis gave rise to contradictory tendencies: toward recentralization on the one hand, toward break-up on the other. But attempts at recentralization reinforced centrifugal tendencies instead of containing them. There were two different types of recentralizing tendencies. The first, pro-free market, took shape behind Croat liberal Ante Markovic, who headed the last Yugoslav government from 1989 on.

The other, "populist" and backward-looking, was identified with the Serbian government of nationalist leader Slobodan Milosevic.[23]

## The market: a force for disintegration

The IMF's precepts encountered considerable resistance during the 1980s. In 1989 Prime Minister Ante Markovic proposed anti-inflation shock therapy (Yugoslavia had triple-digit hyperinflation at the time). This perspective, supported then by the International Monetary Fund and European Community, is often seen today as the lost anti-nationalist, democratic alternative. The democratic currents aligned with Markovic say that his perspective would have made possible a Yugoslavia of citizens, on the foundation of the market and privatizations. This approach had hardly any time to be tried. And the break-up of Yugoslavia along nationalist lines has been such a tragedy that we can easily understand why such an alternative perspective would be seen today as at least a lesser evil.

But there are illusions behind such an approach. To begin with, a promarket perspective would have run into the same problems in Yugoslavia as in the rest of Eastern Europe. There would have been a big risk of having the same impact on the society that shock therapy had in Poland: i.e., some success in the fight against inflation, but at a substantial social cost. Besides, a free market logic could only have deepened the gap, and thus the sociopolitical divergences, between rich and poor regions, as occurred in Czechoslovakia.

Yugoslav promarket policies at the federal level came into direct conflict with promarket policies at the level of the republics: the political stakes and the changes in property forms set Ante Markovic and the leaders of the rich republics in opposition to one another. Slovenian and Croatian leaders wanted to carry out privatizations in a way that would add to their power (by way of a phase of republican government ownership). They wanted to speed up the process of their joining the winners' European Union by cutting themselves free from the poorer republics, which were a brake on the process.

The conflicts were exacerbated with the economic crisis and the most developed republics' growing reluctance to continue funding the federation's budget. For its part, the Serbian government took advantage of the fact that the central bank was in Belgrade, undermining any federal anti-inflation plan. Political differentiation accelerated with the effective break-up of the League of Yugoslav Communists

(LYC) into as many parties as there were republics and provinces, with each party founding its claim to legitimacy on its national policies.

### The pivotal role of the Serb question

In addition to all these problems, there was one issue that would be decisive for any Yugoslav project, given the Serb people's dispersal among several different republics: the rise of Greater-Serbian nationalism. Serb nationalism became a powerful force in 1986, when Slobodan Milosevic became head of the Serbian League of Communists that he had "taken in hand," rebaptizing it the Socialist Party in 1990.[24] The ex-Communists represented the second of the centralizing tendencies mentioned above. *Clearly, they encourage (and justify?) the nationalist turn toward "looking out for number one."* by the republics' governments.

Uprisings had broken out in Kosovo in 1981, at first around socioeconomic issues. Poverty and massive unemployment (20 percent in Kosovo as compared with less than 2 percent in Slovenia at the time) remained the features of this province, whose local bureaucracy had been incompetent managers of the aid Kosovo received.[25] Tensions between the Albanian majority and the Slav minority intensified under the pressure of socioeconomic difficulties and because of the cultural clash between two communities that did not mix. The Kosovo question would be the spark for a flaming up of Serb nationalism *that was breaking decisively with "Titoism."*

Anti-Albanian racism stirrred up Serbs' hatred and fear instead of focusing their discontent on the real deficiencies in every aspect of the province's administration. As in the current war, the media played a decisive role in developing a veritable climate of hysteria. Rape—in Kosovo as later elsewhere—was suddenly denounced, when such denunciations were useful to a national cause: *Albanian* rapes of Serb women were supposedly part of a policy of "ethnic cleansing" aimed at making Serbs flee the Albanian province.[26]

A state of siege was imposed by tanks rolling in. After bloody confrontations with striking Kosovo miners, who demanded the application of the 1974 constitution and free elections, the two provinces were deprived of their autonomy in 1989. Politicians under the Serbian government's thumb took part in the federal collective presidency in Kosovo's and Voivodina's name, compounding the presidency's paralysis. Out of the eight votes assigned to the six republics and two provinces, Slobodan Milosevic could control Montenegro's and the two provinces' in addition to Serbia's. Each representative kept his (there never was a her) right of veto; but on the eve of the declarations of independence, the "Serbian bloc" declared a state of siege throughout Yugoslavia.

This was the end of the Titoist heritage. One of the keys to Titoism's longevity had been, not "anti-Serb" policies, but the rejection of *Serb domination*. The restoration of Serb domination had now begun.

The Yugoslav project had drawn its strength and its *raison d'être* from three main objectives:

— *The fight against the foreign oppressor* (the great powers before World War I; the fascist forces' occupying armies during World War II; the Stalinist Kremlin). The policy of "nonalignment," whatever its ambiguities, drew on a similar, pragmatic resistance to the dictates imposed on the Yugoslav system and its choices by first one and then the other cold war "camp." But toward the end of the 1980s there was no longer any "common foreign enemy." Germany was a pole of attraction for some, a source of worry for others. "Gorbachevism" had put an end to the threat of Soviet tanks.[27] Finally, nonalignment went into crisis with the collapse of one of the blocs. At the same time Yugoslavia lost its importance for the Western world.

— *The common management of human and material resources.* This made a real economic take-off possible for the country. But in a system marked by very great regional (and thus also national) inequalities, openness and evenhanded relationships are the preconditions for success. These the single-party regime lacked, in spite of the progress made. The initial difficulties were real, given the relative advantages that the rich regions had accumulated or inherited through their history and geography. Demographic and cultural differences were also important. Market decentralization in the 1960s contributed in the end to deepening gaps between different sectors and regions. The overall crisis in the 1980s and the shock of pro-market policies functioned as further forces for disintegration, by increasing inequalities and promoting a spirit of "looking out for number one."

— *Rapprochement among national communities that were scattered across a landscape that was ethnically very mixed.* This is a key motive for an attempt at a federal or confederal union. But the project of a union could not be realized politically without a vision of solidarity on the economic level. On the other hand, the borders of Yugoslavia may not have been the optimal limits for resolving the sum of national questions affecting it: today more than ever, relations with Albania, Bulgaria, and Greece are essential to any lasting political solution of intra-Yugoslav conflicts. The issue of peoples' rights, of self-determination, is an explosive one for the vast, mixed Balkan region.

The crisis of the second Yugoslavia could result in a critical evaluation of Titoism, which could serve to found a new union. This was not the dynamic of the 1980s, for reasons that are deeply political and economic.

## Disparities Between Republics
## 1990 (by percent)

|  | Population | Social product per capita* | Agricultural production | Exports | Imports |
|---|---|---|---|---|---|
| Yugoslavia | 100 | 100 | 100 | 100 | 100 |
| Slovenia | 8.1 | 212 | 7.6 | 28.8 | 25.2 |
| Croatia | 19.8 | 123 | 21.3 | 20.5 | 23.6 |
| Serbia | 41.6 | | | | |
| *Minus Provinces* | 24.6 | 93 | 25.3 | 20.8 | 21.2 |
| *Voivodina* | 8.6 | 119 | 23.8 | 8.3 | 11.5 |
| *Kosovo* | 8.3 | 31 | 4.2 | 1.3 | 1.1 |
| Bosnia-Herzegovina | 18.9 | 74 | 9.4 | 14.4 | 6.1 |
| Montenegro | 2.8 | 78 | 1.1 | 1.6 | 1.2 |
| Macedonia | 8.9 | 66 | 7.3 | 4.1 | 6.1 |

*Source:* Yugoslavia Annual Statistics for 1991. See *Le Courrier des Pays de l'Est* no. 364, November 1991, "La Yougoslavie en guerre: le potentiel économique."
* *Social Product per capita* consists of material production plus services linked to production.

# 3

# Wars Within the War

> **The Yugoslav Crisis: Key Dates**
>
> **1981** Violent protests in Kosovo demand a separate republic.
> **1983** IMF-type austerity plan provokes strike waves.
> **1986** Slobodan Milosevic becomes Serbian Communist leader. Serbian Academy of Sciences drafts nationalist Memorandum.
> **1987** Milosevic consolidates power in Serbia.
> **1988** Milosevic extends power in Montenegro and Voivodina. Strikes, protests, and purges in Kosovo.
> **1989** *January:* New Ante Markovic government launches "shock therapy."
> *March:* Serbia challenges Kosovo's and Voivodina's autonomy.
> **1990** *January:* Last Yugoslav Communist congress breaks up in disagreement.
> *March:* State of emergency in Kosovo.
> *April-May:* Elections in Slovenia and Croatia. Tudjman's anti-communist HDZ wins in Croatia.
> *June:* Serbia suspends Kosovo's government and parliament.
> *July:* Secret Kosovo deputies' meeting declares separate republic.
> *November-December:* New Croatian constitution changes Croatian Serbs' status. Elections in Macedonia, Bosnia, Serbia, and Montenegro. Referendum on independence in Slovenia.
> **1991** *March:* Tudjman and Milosevic meet to plan partition of Bosnia. Armed conflicts break out in Croatia: first deaths occur.
> *May:* Serb Krajina votes in referendum for separation from Croatia. Referendum on sovereignty in Croatia.
> *June:* Slovenia and Croatia declare independence. Yugoslav army intervenes in Slovenia.

> *July:* European Community begins arms embargo. Army begins withdrawal from Slovenia; purges and desertions.
> *September:* Referendum on sovereignty in Macedonia. UN Security Council adopts arms embargo.
> *October:* War spreads to one third of Croatia. "Serb bloc" takes over Yugoslav collective presidency. Bosnian parliament votes for sovereignty.
> *December:* Germany recognizes Slovenian and Croatian independence.
> **1992** *January:* Rest of European Community recognizes Slovenia and Croatia.

## FROM CRISIS TO CONSTRUCTION OF EXCLUSIVE NATION-STATES

We have emphasized the strength of centrifugal forces at the end of the crisis-ridden 1980s. But there were also forces working against disintegration: the republics most threatened by the prospect of Yugoslavia's break-up, for one; the ethnically mixed populations, for another. Even in republics where there were referendums on "sovereignty," it was far from clear that people who voted in favor meant to reject Yugoslavia outright. The nationalist regimes may even have needed the war in order to subject their peoples to a dynamic of fear, hatred, and separation, and not just in Bosnia-Herzegovina.[1]

The Croatian referendum was formulated as a choice, not between independence and Yugoslavia, but between federalism and a union of sovereign states (and independence only if the attempt at forming a union failed). The Croatian Serbs did not vote "nationalist" at first—at first they voted "Yugoslav" by supporting ex-Communists. It was Tudjman's campaign that pushed them to vote for Serb nationalists. Even in Slovenia, in whose 1990 referendum people chose independence the most explicitly, their uneasiness was manifested in public opinion polls in the days before June 21, 1991, the date of the Slovenian declaration of independence. After one year in office, Slovenia's new, center-right government was already in crisis and facing a major recession.

The causes of Yugoslavia's socioeconomic fragmentation were powerful, but people were also aware of the risks. It was still possible in 1990-1991 to push forward with dialogues, and make sure that a pluralist debate took place in the media. On the international level it was possible to bring representatives of non-nationalist parties to the negotiating table, and to send observers to republics that were potential "trouble spots"—*before* war broke out.

But in Slovenia and Croatia, as in Serbia, a climate of intellectual terrorism descended, directed against "bad Slovenes" and "bad Croats" much as it had been directed earlier against "bad Serbs." The crisis of "Yugoslavism" was bound to encourage attempts to realize "centuries-old dreams": building nation-states.

The issue was not relations among "ethnic groups" but political and socioeconomic dynamics. The governments of the richest republics (Slovenia and Croatia) wanted to "dump" the rest (as they said in Czechoslovakia to describe the rich region's desire to shake off the burden of the poor region). Serbia, having given up on recentralizing Yugoslavia for its own profit, speeded up its destruction in order to carve a Greater Serbia out of it (stretching all the way to Dubrovnik?) that would make up for its economic weakness. A war in the media prepared a war for land and resources, exploiting national divisions past and present, playing on popular fears in a climate of crisis and uncertainty. But there were other Yugoslav nations who did not have the same chances of gathering up crumbs from the Yugoslav cake by "slicing off" countries.

### *Building nation-states: who profits?*

The negotiations continued until June 1991. But for the Slovenian, Croatian, and Serbian governments, the game was already up. Slovenia and Croatia advocated a confederal or asymmetrical project in which in fact there would have been no common state left: separate armies, separate currencies (the first bills were designed as early as 1990[2]), separate foreign embassies and UN delegations. The Serbian government rejected this proposal, finding it unacceptable without a redrawing of frontiers between the new countries. At the same time Serbia defended its own preference for a federative Yugoslav project, knowing that Slovenia and Croatia would never accept it.

The different political evolutions of the Slovenian and Serbian Communist parties (with the Slovenians heading in a liberal, social democratic direction and the Serbians heading in a repressive, populist direction) accelerated the breaking off of any dialogue, against the backdrop of economic gaps mentioned earlier. Slobodan Milosevic's regime helped erode whatever appeal the idea of federation had left, speeding up Yugoslavia's break-up. But each of the governments intended to build "its own" (Slovene, Serb, or Croat) state. Could the other communities do the same? The conditions for "nation-building" *on an ethnic basis* were not the same (and thus nation-building did not have the same results) in the other republics.

The Serb question was the central issue for the "Yugoslav space," to borrow Yvan Djuric's expression. But given the system's overall crisis, the main, initial dividing line came between those who had the means to create a nation-state on an ethnic basis, in the name of self-determination, and those who had fewer or no means to do so.

On one side of the dividing line were Serbia, Croatia, and Slovenia. On the other side we have to put the "minorities" who were not granted the right to self-determination, beginning with the Albanians, and those we might call the "uncertain" nations: above all those who felt themselves to be "Bosnians" or Macedonians, peoples who lived on much-coveted lands. Since they were recognized as "nations," they enjoyed in theory the same rights as Serbs, Croats, and Slovenes; but in practice they were less clearly "marked off," more "impure," more contested and fragile.

The fact that the Montenegrins were ethnically very close to the Serbs made it easier for them to stay together with Serbia. But their very closeness to the Serbs is felt more and more as a danger for Montenegro's future, a threat of "assimilation." So Montenegro can also be ranked among the "uncertains," the ones with a contested identity.

Bosnia-Herzegovina and Macedonia were the most threatened, politically and economically, by Yugoslavia's fragmentation. It is no accident then that their representatives were much more interested than the others in finding a compromise that would keep some kind of union together, whatever the cost. Together they developed a compromise proposal: a union at several different speeds, more "confederative" for Slovenia and Croatia, more binding for the others. There would have been both a common state (with embassies and a UN delegation, an army and a monetary system) and forms of international representation for republics with their own national armies, with a strict limitation of the central government's powers.

These proposals were rejected by the other protagonists, beginning with the Serbian government. But if Serbia had been the only one in favor of a break, a completely different relationship of forces could have taken shape—particularly because the army still looked positively on any Yugoslav project. Since the real aim in Slovenia, Serbia, and Croatia was to build nation-states, this raised the problem of "ethnic frontiers."

### *Non-ethnic frontiers*

The borders between republics were obviously not going to be accepted in the absence of the overall balance that Yugoslavia had represented. The issue of the borders between republics was organically tied to the federation's borders and to each of the republics' constitutional self-definition.

The republics that had been the scene of the worst conflicts in the past had in fact been explicitly defined as multinational, in this sense meaning multiethnic. Given the history of forced assimilation and genocide, this definition was obviously meant to protect minorities. But not all conflicts were treated everywhere in the same constitutional way. In Serbia there were provinces, corresponding to the "minorities"; but the Serb minority in Croatia had no province. The Serbs were not assigned any territory in Croatia because they were mixed together with Croats in the cities, and also because they did not have "minority" status. Croatia was defined (before the adoption of the December 1990 constitution) as the country of the Croat "people" (or ethnic nation) *and* as that of the Croatian Serb "people" as well as the other communities' (national minorities') country, without the Serbs ever putting forward any particular demand for territorial autonomy.

The same was true of the three peoples making up Bosnia-Herzegovina. The Bosnian Muslim, Serb, and Croat communities were put on the same level irrespective of their numbers; they were not assigned to "ethnic provinces" (because no region or territory was homogeneous). In other words, the peoples of Croatia and Bosnia-Herzegovina were treated in a similar way. The only difference was that there was an absolute Croat majority in Croatia, which fostered a feeling of "frustrated sovereignty" among Croat nationalists. By contrast there was no absolute majority in Bosnia. This fact fostered a multiethnic approach among the Muslim community, which had a relative majority.

As soon as Yugoslavia broke apart and governments aiming at independent countries predominated, the question of the right to self-determination was posed.

### Self-determination "of peoples" or of republics?

The right to self-determination was recognized in the Yugoslav constitution. But only the "nations" were granted this right; it was denied to the Albanians. Besides, how could this right be applied to peoples scattered across several republics: on what territorial base, through what procedures?

Before Slovenia's June 1991 declaration of independence, its president, Milan Kucan, signed along with Milosevic a pact confirming the right to self-determination as a principle applicable to (ethnic) "peoples." For the geographically concentrated Slovenes, this meant more or less their own, relatively homogeneous republic; everywhere else in Yugoslavia, it meant conflict.

The Croatian government began by counterposing to self-determination of *peoples* a conception based on *republics*. Since ethnic Croats make up 80 percent of the Croatian republic's population, applying majority rule could guarantee a vote for independence, and turn the Croatian Serbs into an ethnic minority. Croatian policy in Bosnia-Herzegovina (where Croats are in a minority) falls back nonetheless on the principle of ethnically based nation-building and territorial division, just like Serbian policy. And in Serbia the Serbs impose their own rules on their minorities. In other words, the Serbian and Croatian governments install majority rule where it suits them and consider it unacceptable elsewhere.

According to the Yugoslav constitution, the federation's or republics' borders could only be changed by consensus. The procedural debate during the crisis of the system counterposed the Slovenian and Croatian conception of referendums, done republic by republic on questions formulated by the republican governments, to the conceptions of the Yugoslav head of government Ante Markovic and the Serbian leader Slobodan Milosevic. Markovic and Milosevic proposed unified procedures directed at all of Yugoslavia's inhabitants as a body, so that Yugoslavs could respond as citizens and as people claiming a specific nationality; conflicts, according to Markovic and Milosevic, should be worked out by consensus.

So Slovenia's and Croatia's unilateral declarations of independence were denounced as illegal, not only by the Serbian government but also by the (last) Yugoslav prime minister, Ante Markovic.[3]

## *Toward Greater Serbia*

To Milosevic these separations were irreversible facts, and as such he hardly challenged them. The Serbian government had doubtless given up on Yugoslavia as early as the end of the 1980s: the 1986 Memorandum of the Serbian Academy of Sciences, which inspired Milosevic's policies, analyzed the crisis of the Yugoslav system and the growing paralysis of the federation.

The Memorandum was not an appeal to "purify the race." On the other hand, it clearly announced that Serbs would "take back Serb sovereignty over Serbia": abolishing Kosovo's and Voivodina's autonomy would be the first step in the creation of Greater Serbia. The document defended "Serbs' right to be brought together in a single state" and to protect the Serb diaspora from "new dangers of genocide." "'Preventive vengeance': that is the true program of Serb nationalism."[4]

This Greater Serbian project was most explicitly defended by Vuk Draskovic's Party of Serb Renewal (in the opposition) and by Vojislav Seselj's Radical Party, which was allied with Slobodan Milosevic at the time. For a long time this alliance made it possible for Milosevic to confine himself officially to pro-Yugoslav rhetoric; refrain from officially recognizing the self-proclaimed Serb republics in Croatia and Bosnia-Herzegovonia (while declaring his solidarity with Serbs' right to self-determination); and leave the dirty work to extreme right militias protected and supplied by the army.

In practice Belgrade supported the creation of the self-proclaimed republics. But the Serbian government has continued nonetheless to have a position distinct from those of the Croatian and Bosnian Serb leaders. For one thing, the Serbian government is more directly subject to international pressure. But it also has to contend with the danger of seeing the same separatism applied to Kosovo that Serbs are championing in Croatia and Bosnia-Herzegovina. Bosnia-Herzegovina's confederalization, or worse its complete break-up, could only heighten the pressures pushing in the same direction in Serbia and Croatia.[5]

The official rhetoric advocated *the Serb people's right to continue living in a single country,* if not in Yugoslavia then some other country; not, as has sometimes been said, a rejection of Croat self-determination. But the same right of self-determination would later be denied to the Bosnians. It was denied to the Albanians as well during the creation of the first Yugoslavia. A people split between several different countries, the Albanians became after 1918 a "minority" in Yugoslavia, as the Serbs of Croatia and Bosnia-Herzegovina have abruptly become today.

As for Serb self-determination: the Serb populations were never consulted about any such project (the Memorandum was not a public document). Still less was there a debate: press and television were made to march in step, broadcasting images of horrors drawn from World War II (supposedly in order to prepare for the next war). By all accounts, it was the militias that set the machinery of fear and violence in motion. The support given the militias by the Serbian government and the army would be an essential element in the striking power and impunity of these criminal militiamen.

### *The Yugoslav army: pro-Serb?*

Historian Yvan Djuric reminds us:

> Few people realized in late June 1991 that the Serbian government was only encouraging Slovenia's secession. Serbia wanted to make the federal army leave Slovenian territory. It hoped, rightly, that Croatia, seen as Serbia's real enemy in the war, would thus be made particularly vulnerable politically.[6]

We can even add that several analysts presented the army's intervention in Slovenia quite differently, and wrongly, as a "Greater Serbian" act.

In any event, the Yugoslav army's intervention, after the Slovenian government's decision to establish border controls, produced a radical swing in favor of independence among the republic's population.[7] But the "phony war" in Slovenia was not the kind of war that would happen later, first in Croatia and then in Bosnia-Herzegovina. The Slovenian "war" can be characterized as the Yugoslav army's (last) intervention against an act of Slovenian self-determination. The war in Croatia and Bosnia-Herzegovina has a different logic. By the time war broke out in Croatia, the army had already suffered the immediate repercussions of its defeat in Slovenia: from that point on there was no longer any question of keeping Yugoslavia together. The army intervened in Croatia in the name of Serb self-determination, not against Croat self-determination. At the same time, intervention in Croatia served the ends of Greater Serbian expansionism.

But we should discuss the first war first. At the moment that the signs were being changed along Slovenia's borders, the Yugoslav collective presidency—the army's commander-in-chief, constitutionally speaking—was paralyzed. There was only one federal, Yugolav authority left, the government led by Croat liberal Ante Markovic. Slovenia's minister of defense accused Markovic of encouraging the army's intervention. Markovic's statements threatening action against any nonconsensual changing of Yugoslav frontiers[8] were in fact all the firmer because they were backed at the time by the "international community," which defended the inviolability of frontiers as a basic principle.[9] All this was bound at least to encourage the army to intervene, even if its general staff tended to act autonomously and play a political role in the crisis. For those who see only a single, Serb aggressor at work everywhere, perhaps even mentioning this somehow "dilutes Serbia's responsibility" for unleashing the war.

The Yugoslav army was defending its privileges and the federation—not any Greater Serbian project (yet).[10] Its tradition was "Titoist," not "Greater Serbian": statistics about officers' ethnicity do not reflect this fact. By this hypothesis, the officers' political orientation served, not their ethnicity, but the material interests defended by the general staff. In addition, ideological dimensions became secondary in this period of crisis, even if part of the army command supported the founding of a new Party of Yugoslav Communists.[11] The army's material interests and *raison d'être* were tied to the preservation of a Yugoslav state. In those times of crisis, that was the essential detail.

The army's relationship with Slobodan Milosevic was conflictual, since Serb nationalism was rightly seen as threatening the integrity of the Yugoslav state. As Branko Horvat says about it:

> At the time of the eighth session[12] the Yugoslav army opposed Milosevic, and often acted to prevent mutual killing sprees. It had been formed above all as a *Yugoslav* army.[13]

From this standpoint the army, whose general staff respected the Titoist system's "ethnic key" of equilibrium between nationalities, was doubtless divided in 1989-1991. But at least a significant part of the general staff leaned more toward supporting Ante Markovic than toward a Serb nationalist project that would tend to pull Yugoslavia apart.

A "phony war," we call this intervention in Slovenia: because many things about it are still unclear, and the picture given by the media is very far from the facts on the ground. *Six deaths among the Slovenian population, several dozen in the army*: the figures themselves pose questions to anyone who wants to think. Disarmed soldiers (disarmed in every sense of the word) were sent, not to fight, but to protect the frontiers against the "danger of foreign intervention" (*sic*)![14]

Was this intervention done out of naiveté? Was it a manipulation or a mistake made by an army that was overconfident that redeploying a few tanks would be enough to "restore order"? It certainly came up against an efficient "Slovenian Territorial Defense."[15] Unlike its Croatian counterpart, the Slovenian Territorial Defense had managed to hinder the recentralization of military supplies undertaken by the Yugoslav army as the crisis intensified. In any case, the Yugoslav army's general staff refused explicitly in front of the television cameras to be labeled a "foreign occupying force" or to play this role. It very quickly decided (by the summer of 1991) to withdraw from Slovenia.

This episode served as a catalyst for a purge and a radicalization of Serb nationalist forces inside the Yugoslav army. From this moment we can date the army's qualitative leap toward the only government that wanted it: the Serbian government. This did not mean that the Serbian government and Yugoslav army had identical interests, nor that the army was homogeneous. Recent purges show a continuing polarization. When Milan Panic[16] opposed Milosevic for the Serbian presidency, for example, several officers of the general staff were suspected of supporting Panic.

Apart from the candidate, it is reasonable to think that part of the army is interested first of all in its job security and privileges: i.e. stabilization and international recognition of the new Yugoslav federation (Serbia plus Montenegro). So part of the army can back the pragmatic Milosevic when he breaks with his extremists in order to consolidate the new state. Another part of the army instead backs Vojislav Seselj's radical Greater Serbia project. Some of the officers jailed for corruption in Banja Luka in Bosnia during the September

1993 uprising seem to have been Seselj supporters. Anyway Seselj was certainly looking for support among diaspora Serbs.

## Constitutional changes in Serbia and Croatia

The Serbian and Croatian governments each amended its constitution in a parallel way. The constitutional changes in Croatia echo the changes in Kosovo: they go *in the same direction*, with only a few juridical variations. Serbian and Croatian policies are similar—produced by the same crisis and the same aspirations toward dismemberment of Yugoslavia on an ethnic basis—although there are also differences, beginning with the Greater Serbian project's more brutal violence.

Under Tito's constitution Serb sovereignty had gone no further than the borders of the autonomous provinces, Kosovo and Voivodina; Slobodan Milosevic abolished and repressed the provinces' autonomy (while defining Serbia as "the state of all its citizens," without reference to the Serb ethnic nation). Sovereignty in Croatia had been shared by "the Croat people and the Serb people of Croatia": the new Croatian government eliminated the second part of the phrase. The rights of minorities were reaffirmed, of course, and citizenship is theoretically broader than the ethnic nation. The step backward can be seen in historical context, however, relative to the previous texts, and on the ground, in both Kosovo and Croatia. The facts on the ground explain the perception of these changes by the main groups concerned, and their reactions.

In Kosovo, the Albanians have lost all the political and cultural autonomy given them by the 1974 constitution. They are subject to a government imposed from Belgrade and to a policy that aims officially at the "Serbization" of the province (even if this policy is failing). The results: tens of thousands of Albanians laid off, while Serb refugees have been incited to come and take their jobs; police pressures and constant provocations; name changes for schools and streets; bans on teaching in Albanian; a policy of apartheid; pillage of the province's resources through cut-rate privatization to the benefit of Serb companies; eviction from apartments; suppression or harassment of the Albanian-language press—and an exodus of Albanians from Kosovo.

And the Croatian Serbs? "The ones that are left, you mean!" exclaims the Croat Ivan Zvonimir Cicak, member of the Helsinki Human Rights Commission, imprisoned for Croat nationalism under

Tito's regime, and founder in 1990 of the Croat Peasants Party (which he has since left).

This "bad Croat" explains the workings of

> planned ethnic cleansing in Croatia through blowing up houses from the inside; laying Serbs off; confiscating their homes; denying them Croatian nationality (which means depriving them of most of their rights); abusing them; and using the media to create a climate of psychotic persecution.[17]

Out of 500,000 refugees in Serbia and Montenegro, 80 percent are Serbs; about 200,000 come from Croatia. The most recent waves of refugees come not from areas at war or where there are open conflicts, but from the big cities.

The concern expressed recently by Croatian Jews at the rehabilitation of notorious Croat fascists[18] should open people's eyes about a government that Croatian society is beginning to reject.

## SHARED BUT UNEQUAL RESPONSIBILITIES

Against a background of crisis and of economic policies deepening the gap between rich and less developed republics, war is not an "interethnic struggle." It serves the purpose of the dominant nations' governments: to build nation-states over ex-Yugoslavia's dead body, using ethnicity as a basis of legitimation and a pretext for grabbing resources—including territories.

Yugoslavia's entire constitutional equilibrium, with its carefully calibrated national rights, has collapsed in this process. So the war also involves real conflicts and difficulties about how to apply self-determination in an exploding multiethnic country with ethnically mixed republics.

The fact that the newly independent countries are ruled by undemocratic governments displaces the problem. These governments' ends must be judged by their means: threatened minorities, killings, populations under siege in the cities, rape and other humiliations, all inflicted in order to instill fear, to spur to flight, to "cleanse" territories.

It was important to discuss what was responsible for the crisis and fragmentation. But then *who* is responsible for the war? The carrying out of the Serb nationalist project affects all the republics where Serbs are to be found. It risks setting off new violence in Kosovo and then spreading as well to Macedonia. Because the Serbs were Yugoslavia's largest nationality, the Serb question plays a pivotal role. The Serbian government's ability to use the old Yugoslav state apparatus—its currency and above all its army—also gave it a central responsibility for unleashing the violence. In a war the question "Who shot first?" clarifies certain sequences of events, but it is not enough to explain the nature of the problems at hand.

Serbian policy has a clearly "preventive" dimension. Serbian paranoia doubtless accelerated, even set off what it was supposedly meant to forestall: the break-up of the federation, the threats to Serb citizenship in Croatia, Germany's rearmament of Croatia, the rise of Muslim fundamentalism (which would actually take place in the end). But Serbian policy did not cause the fragmentation of Yugoslavia all by itself. The war served several different ends. There has been a synergistic effect—if not actual complicity—among the various nationalist-oriented governments.

*This is why we can speak of joint but unequal responsibilities.*

*Unequal* because, due to the alliances described above, the military relationship of forces enabled the partisans of the Greater Serbian project to impose their point of view by force. Bombs fell on Croatian and Bosnian territory, not on Serbian territory, because of this imbalance of forces that was there from the beginning.

*Unequal* also because not all nationalities were in the same situation in ex-Yugoslavia, either in the crisis or in attempts to build nation-states on an ethnic basis. There were the recognized, solidly established nations and then there were the others, the weaker ones, and the Albanian "minority" that was not recognized as a people at all. The Serbs and Croats in Bosnia-Herzegovina each have a country outside Bosnia-Herzegovina that is a reference point for them; the Muslim community of Bosnia-Herzegovina has only Bosnia-Herzegovina. The fact that national identities are more mixed and subject to questioning in Bosnia and Macedonia make these republics the victims of choice for the dominant nationalisms which reject any kind of union. For Bosnia and Macedonia their unilateral declarations of independence were agonized choices. But the coming to power of nationalist parties in Bosnia made the country ungovernable.

> The Kosovo crisis was a turning point in this process. But the unity of the country no longer existed, and other republics' leaders declared that Kosovo was an internal Serbian affair.[19]

Kosovo basically remained an "internal Serbian affair" because the Slovenian government did not want to "support" Yugoslavia's less developed regions, and because the Croatian government meant the change in Croatian Serbs' status to be an "internal Croatian affair."

Greater Serbian projects drew sustenance from projects of a similar nature in Croatia, even if the Croat projects were not formulated as bluntly. Croatian President Franjo Tudjman's rejection of "Yugoslavism" boiled down to an ethnic conception of citizenship. In periods of crisis, when the memory of dark moments of the past comes back to life, symbolic acts are important. Eliminating Victims of Fascism Square in Zagreb by renaming it Great Croats Square; declaring, "I'm happy that my wife is neither a Serb nor a Jew" (as Tudjman did in Croatia); amending the constitution in a provocative way—all these acts gave rise to real fear among Croatian Serbs and fostered extremism, quite apart from anything contrived by the Belgrade government.

In this connection we have to distinguish nationalism of the "higher-ups" (which aims at controlling and conquering resources and territories) with nationalism of the "lower-downs," whose main moving force is fear. In order for the (undeniable) manipulation of popular fears to "work," there have to have been real traumas in the past and there have to be equally real uncertainties or threats in the present. This is what has to be understood and dealt with in order to take away extremist nationalism's mass base.

Croatian Serb Milorad Pupovac—simultaneously a "bad Croat" and a "bad Serb," since he is critical of both Greater Serbian and Greater Croatian policies—is noteworthy for his lack of bias:

> The Croatian Serbs find themselves afraid of the people among whom they must live; and the Croats find themselves suspicious of the Croatian Serbs! This double vise-grip in which Croatian Serbs are living has tragic consequences. [They] are divided to begin with between those who cling to the idea of fictitious Croatian Serb statelets—founded in a moment of fear, turbulence, and violence—and those who live, with no political rights, physically threatened, without legal protection, in areas under Croatian authority. They have in addition militarized themselves, jumped several centuries back into the past... thrown themselves into activities unworthy of civilized human beings—or they are prey to defeatism and despair. Croatian Serbs are still cut off by an abyss of suspicion that is all the deeper because it has two causes: their share of responsibility

for Serbia's territorial demands on Croatia, and Croatia's responsibility for its war against Croatian Serbs.[20]

Greater Croatian policies (whether they involve greater or smaller ambitions in Bosnia-Herzegovina) have been hypocritical, but have been scarcely denounced in the media because they have been hidden behind doubletalk about Bosnia-Herzegovina. They have been hidden behind Croat nationalists' posturing as "democratic" victims of "Serbo-Communism," while all along Croatia has been negotiating with "Serbo-Communism" in the corridors.

### Varieties of extreme right populism

Milosevic's government was heir to a state apparatus with neo-Stalinist characteristics. It consolidated itself by means of purges and a restructuring (in part destruction) of the old "Yugoslav" state. Milosevic's alliance (since broken) with Vojislav Seselj's Radical Party was reminiscent of "red-brown" rapprochements elsewhere. ("Red-brown" refers to alignments in Russia and elsewhere between neo-Stalinist currents and fascist-leaning nationalist parties—"browns," after the Nazi "brown shirts.") But the "red" party (Milosevic's) has little to do with Tito, and considers the Comintern the source of all the Serbs' ills. As for the "brown" party (Seselj's), it lays claim to the Chetnik tradition. The Chetniks were at least theoretically antifascist and proroyalist: today's Chetniks are fighting in the name of the "anti-Ustashe" struggle.[21]

In other words, both sides come off as "fascist." It is clear in any case that a major difference with World War II is that now there is no foreign invader. But even if the fight against the occupation is over, the methods remain. In this area the Chetnik groups do not need any lessons from fascists. Milosevic's break with Seselj's party since late September 1993 does not necessarily mean that he has renounced violent methods: "Arkan's" militias[22] are state-run institutions which were devoted to Milosevic's government for a long time, even if Milosevic now prefers to keep the alliance less visible than before or even break it in order to seem more respectable abroad.

The Croatian regime for its part broke very early with the "Ustashe" extreme right that was tarnishing its image. It has often boasted that the Ustashe received a smaller share of the vote than Jean-Marie LePen's National Front in France or than Seselj in Serbia (at the time when Milosevic was his ally). Croatia has nonetheless relied on its status as "Serbo-Communist victim" in order to cover up a centralist approach and "ethnic cleansing" no less disturbing than Serbia's—even if carried out with less publicity and less international condemnation. Control over the media was more absolute in Zagreb than in Belgrade, at least until the open split in Tudjman's party in 1994.[23]

Emigration (mainly from the United States, Canada, and Australia) has furnished the Croatian state apparatus with extreme right recruits. Defense Minister Gojko Susak is the prototype of a Croat extreme rightist, giving military support to Mate Boban's policies in Bosnia-Herzegovina. These new arrivals are now rubbing shoulders with new and holdover apparachiks. Purges on ethnic and political grounds have had the same character in Croatia as in Kosovo, affecting first Serbs and now, massively, Bosnians.

In both Serbia and Croatia the authoritarian regimes have relied on parliamentary forms. Their opponents describe them as "dictocracies": dictatorships wrapped in the forms of democracy. Both Milosevic and Tudjman tolerate the existence of trade unions—some of which are genuinely independent from the government, like Nezavisnost in Serbia—and antiwar movements and civic organizations. In both Serbia and Croatia natalist programs are tending to put in question women's right to control their own bodies.[24] "Large-scale manipulation of women ('mothers') by nationalists on all sides was a source of happiness for both sides' fighters," Rada Ivekovic emphasizes. "The nationalist 'reconquest' of women was a fact." There was also a "reconquest" of rape, a crime that was denounced only when denunciation served a national cause. At the same time, however, peace, antifascist, and humanitarian movements are overwhelmingly composed of women, the first victims of the politics of exclusion.

While the Serbian and Croatian regimes are drifting toward fascism, particularly because of the governments' various moves toward alliance with the extreme right, such alliances are not stable at the moment. Both Milosevic and Tudjman have repeatedly done a balancing act between the various currents they rely on.

# 4

# The Bosnian Symbol

### Main Periods in Bosnian History

**500-600**   Slavs arrive in Bosna river area.
**From 800**   Christian missions reach Balkans from Rome and Constantinople.
**Until 1377**   Serbia, Croatia, Bulgaria, and Hungary fight to control Bosnia.
**1377**   Tvrtko, governor of Bosnia, is crowned as king.

*1463-1878   Ottoman rule*
Islam makes steady, major advances in Bosnia.
**1554**   At first divided into districts, Bosnia becomes a province.
**early 1800s**   Tensions grow between conservative Bosnian officials and reforming Ottoman central government.
**mid-nineteenth century**   Christian serfs revolt against Bosnian Muslim rulers. Serb and Croat nationalism gain influence.
**1878**   Austria-Hungary occupies Bosnia.

*1878-1918   Austro-Hungarian rule*
Muslim officials preserve their privileges.
**1908**   Austria-Hungary annexes Bosnia. Orthodox and Muslims get political and cultural autonomy.
**1914**   Assassination of Austrian archduke begins World War I.

> **1918-1945**  *The first Yugoslavia*
> **1929** Bosnia completely loses political status inside Yugoslavia.
> **1941-1945** World War II: Bosnia is absorbed into Greater Croatia.
>
> **1945-1991** *Tito's Yugoslavia*
> **1945** Bosnia becomes a republic within its historic frontiers.
> **1974** Last Yugoslav constitution defines Bosnia as state of three equal peoples: Muslim, Serb, and Croat.

## IS BOSNIA-HERZEGOVINA ARTIFICIAL?

The international negotiators are more and more inclined to organize the break-up of Bosnia-Herzegovina, while preserving the integrity of Croatia and Serbia. Nevertheless Bosnia-Herzegovina is no more "an artificial creation" than Yugoslavia was, or than each of the countries that has emerged from Yugoslavia's fragmentation. Just like Serbia and Croatia, Bosnia-Herzegovina has in its medieval past a precursor state—called Bosnia. Its current frontiers may be more "historical" than those of any other ex-Yugoslav countries, and it "constituted an autonomous administrative unit throughout the long period of Ottoman occupation (fifteenth to nineteenth centuries) as well as, more recently, the period of Austro-Hungarian occupation (1878-1918)."[1]

Bosnia-Herzegovina disappeared into the administrative divisions established within the first Yugoslavia ruled by the Serb dynasty, then was absorbed into the Ustashe's Greater Croatia. But it was one of the areas of greatest resistance to fascism. The Partisan general staff set up its headquarters there, and laid the foundations there for the second, federative Yugoslavia. It was one of the new federation's constituent republics: besides having in and of itself many claims to this status, within Tito's logic it provided a means to balance the relationship of forces between Serb and Croat nationalism.

It was thus in the front ranks of republics threatened with death by Yugoslavia's fragmentation and by the logic of building ethnically pure countries in Serbia and Croatia. As Xavier Bougarel reminds us,

> If Bosnia-Herzegovina has one distinctive and enduring feature, it consists in belonging to no one people, in being a permanent site of intermingling and assimilation, a crossroads of civilizations and a periphery of empires.[2]

Is a country without a dominant (ethnic) people therefore an unviable country, without a soul, a society without history or cohesion?

### *The Bosnian blend*

The republic's ethnic and social composition has gone through major upheavals in the last several decades. In 1971 a shift was registered in the demographic pattern that had existed since after World War II. The Serbs, previously a relative majority of the population, now constituted no more than a third, while the Muslims (who from this time on could identify themselves as such within the census' ethnic categories) were more than 40 percent. (The Croats constituted 18 percent.)

Xavier Bougarel divides Bosnian municipalities into five categories according to their degree of ethnic mixture.[3] In 1991, less than 10 percent of the population lived in "homogeneous" municipalities (those in which a single group made up 80 percent of the population). In addition, a growing majority (about 60 percent) of Bosnians lived in bipolar municipalities. While 74.2 percent of Bosnian Serbs lived in Serb-majority municipalities in 1948, by 1991 only 50.2 percent lived in Serb-majority municipalities.[4]

In any event the ethnic map only gives a very rough idea of the republic's real complexity. Urban areas do not all have the same majority as the rural areas around them; what takes the form of intermingling in cities is often juxtaposition of unmixed villages in the countryside; and finally many individuals and families are of mixed origin, which ethnic maps do not reflect. But the important thing is the *dynamic* of this society: were industrialization, development, and access to culture leading to ethnic rapprochement or to ethnic differentiation?

We have already stressed that the Bosnian population that emerged from Ottoman rule was socially stratified along lines of religious division. In 1910, more than 90 percent of landowners were Muslim, while about 73 percent of agricultural workers (*kmets*) were Orthodox and 20 percent Catholic (less than 5 percent Muslim). Already under the Austro-Hungarian empire, many Muslims settled in cities and became educated. This led to a decrease in the importance of religion, in a community where religious choices included a significant "opportunistic" dimension: self-protection was often more important than belief in conversions. In the great nineteenth century Bosnian families, uncertain whether their future rulers would be Ottoman or Austrian, fathers ordered their children: "You, son, will be a Catholic—and *you* will be a Muslim."

The consequences of the land reforms and Serb rule in the first Yugoslavia manifested themselves after World War II. Serbs remained a majority among the Bosnian peasantry as a whole, but they were a minority among poor peasants and overrepresented among well-off peasants. They predominated in the administration. "Muslims"[5] were by contrast overrepresented in traditional urban occupations (artisans, merchants, private entrepreneurs) and among blue-collar workers.

Several decades later, in the second Yugoslavia, the social gaps had narrowed. The Muslim community had strengthened its position among the republics' managers and intelligentsia: in 1981 about 30 percent of administrators in political and social organizations, legislative bodies, and firms were members of the Muslim community (while Serbs kept a relative majority of 33 to 35 percent). Among the artistic, scientific, and medical intelligentsia the percentages were roughly the same (although Serbs were overrepresented among teachers). Croats' share in all these occupations roughly corresponded to their proportion of the labor force (16.3 percent). A disproportionate number of those working in agriculture continued to be Serbs, while miners were drawn disproportionately from the Muslim community (60.1 percent). Significantly, industrial workers were the only occupation in which the percentages matched the share of the communities in the total population.[6] The decline of religious affiliation was most marked among Muslims and Serbs, less marked among Croats.

The 1990 electoral results in the Tuzla industrial and mining region reflected the ethnic and social reality: non-nationalist parties won a majority there. The region's ethnic composition before the Bosnian war mirrored the republic's (roughly 40 percent in the Muslim community, 30 percent Serbs, and 18 percent Croats).

| Ethnic Composition and Religious Affiliation in Bosnia-Herzegovina 1990 (by percent)[7] |||
|---|---|---|
| Muslim community: | 43.7 | Muslims: 16.5 |
| Serbs: | 31 | Orthodox: 20 |
| Croats: | 17.3 | Catholics: 15 |
|  | | No religious affiliation: 46 |

Xavier Bougarel's study shows that, generally speaking, the "citizen" parties—whether they originated from the League of Yugoslav Communists or its mass organizations or (in the case of the Reformist Party) supported Prime Minister Ante Markovic—did better "in heterogeneous municipalities on the one hand and in Muslim-majority municipalities on the other (reflecting the Muslim national group's less homogeneous voting patterns)."[8]

Now "the most heterogeneous municipalities are generally the most urbanized as well, and those benefitted most from Bosnia-Herzegovina's economic development." The poorest and most religious rural areas were, taken as a whole, the areas where nationalist voting patterns prevailed. For example, eastern Bosnia-Herzegovina is still marked by past confrontations, both those that took place during the Ottoman period and the massacres of the Muslim population during World War II. Herzegovina's Croats have a stronger religious and nationalist identity than Croats in central Bosnia, where the Franciscan monks are also more "Bosnian."

> Posavina, where homogeneous voting patterns were particularly weak, is typical of a nationally heterogeneous region, but it is also a region of relatively prosperous agriculture and early industrialization, marked for many years by its proximity to Austria-Hungary and the ethnically heterogeneous regions of Slavonia and Voivodina.[9]

## *The crisis and nationalist regimes: causes of fragmentation*

These results bear out our general hypothesis: *that there is a positive correlation between commitment to a multiethnic reality, on the one hand, and an economic development resulting in urbanization, industrialization, and intermingling, on the other.* The countryside has often been cut off from these developments. There *komsiluk* (neighborly relations between communities, dating back to the Ottoman empire) meant not so much genuine intermingling as a juxtaposition of cultures and communities tied to different religions. So the countryside is more combustible in times of crisis, from the moment when the forces in power no longer represent the whole of Bosnian society in an indifferentiated way. More vivid memories of the past are undoubtedly important as well in these rural areas (even though the role of the militias and manipulation by the media has played an essential role in bringing suspicions and fears back to life).

In the cities, by contrast, it is *the most recent past* that has the biggest impact on people's consciousness. In Bosnia-Herzegovina, the most recent past *tended toward the creation of a multiethnic "Bosnian" national community, content to live together.* Nationalist logics were rooted in the poorest and most religious social categories and regions.

But the war and ethnic cleansing have been most violent elsewhere: in areas where Serbs (for instance) were in a minority. Precisely because Serb-majority areas were not contiguous, the policy of uniting Serbs in a single country inexorably demands an aggressive dynamic of cutting "ethnic corridors." In the war in Croatia as well, many of the towns conquered and "cleansed" by Serb militias were not Serb-majority areas. The cleansing resulted from the militias' will to build "a country that would hold together," that would be "viable," sometimes by taking control of roads or strategic factories. Croat forces' violent conquest of Mostar fit into this same state-building dynamic.

The causes of disintegration are thus to be found not mainly or first of all in the distant past and its interethnic conflicts (even though such conflicts have sometimes played an important role in some regions), but in the economic crisis and its political consequences: the rise of nationalist currents among the ruling elites, who want to build ethnically based countries on ethnically mixed land. The votes of rural municipalities help explain nationalists' electoral success. But it is neither a sufficient explanation nor even a wholly convincing one (since voting for a "national" party does not necessarily imply support for all its policies).

Xavier Bougarel emphasizes a paradox: "Even though several decades of socialist Yugoslavia put relations between national groups in better balance on the social level, an explosion of nationalist resentments ... marked its end."[10] The paradox obviously disappears for those who think that the war has revealed Bosnia-Herzegovina's hidden reality—interethnic hatred—a reality that Communism supposedly stifled in Bosnia as in the whole of Yugoslavia. Nonetheless, those who seriously examine the real situation find that it does not bear out this supposedly obvious conclusion. Nor is the conclusion confirmed by interviews done among refugees who have fallen victim to "ethnic cleansing": in Bosnia-Herzegovina, as in the mixed Serb-Croat areas of Croatia, the majority of those questioned do not mention any particular conflicts among neighbors before the war, much less explain the war in this way.[11]

This is why seeing things the other way around is more convincing: there is so little "natural" about separation that it was necessary to isolate the towns so that the villages' militias and manipulated mobilizations could silence them; necessary to stir up fears linked to Yugoslavia's break-up itself; necessary to use threatening images in order to resurrect buried memories of the past. It was necessary to humiliate, to terrorize, to commit rape, to destroy the symbols of different identities: not in order to "purify a race" as the media say,[12] but to *clean out territory in order to build states.*

This war is an outcome of the fragmentation of Yugoslavia, an outcome of the ruling nationalist policies in Belgrade and Zagreb—and an outcome of the international crisis of progressive projects. But it finds internal props within Bosnian society, because Bosnian society is necessarily, deeply affected by the overall crisis that has destroyed Yugoslavia. The 1990 electoral results showed the polarizations at work that weakened the Bosnian blend from within.

We have to understand the ways in which the causal chain was simultaneously rational and obscure. On the eve of Bosnia-Herzegovina's elections, all the polls forecast a majority for the non-nationalist parties. Svebor Dizdarevic has recalled in many discussions of these events that the principle of "national" parties had been rejected in polls shortly before the elections, because people were so conscious of the deathly danger that such parties represented in Bosnia-Herzegovina. This sentiment was so widespread that "on election day several national parties, unable to believe that they were actually winning, declared that the elections were being rigged and even called out their supporters for mass demonstrations," Nenad Fiser remembers.[13]

With hindsight we can understand the "ethnic vote" that took place. Reasoning in the context of the prior regime's economic and moral crisis, voters logically pronounced their verdict on the clear failure of the late 1980s by casting a non-Communist vote. In the absence of pluralist traditions, the main opposition parties were recent creations, basing their "programs" on anti-Communism and ethnicity. "A 'pact of honor' was made among them that their respective supporters would vote for non-Communist candidates on all the national lists, and would support one another."[14] Facing this alliance, the opposition proved by contrast to be disunited and incapable of putting forward a coherent (political and socioeconomic) alternative on the level on which Bosnia could actually be defended: the level of Yugoslavia as a whole.

Subsequently the three nationalist parties (the Serb SDS, the Croat HDZ, and SDA for the Muslim community) promised during the electoral campaign to govern jointly—and initially they did (dividing up the top positions). The "ethnic vote" in the first elections can thus be interpreted as a vote to punish those responsible for the crisis and as an (illusory) safeguard against Bosnia's break-up. The ethnic vote only embraced 55 percent of the electorate anyway; 25 percent voted for non-nationalist parties and 20 percent abstained. So it cannot be said that these elections expressed a popular will for separation.

The vote for independence was a choice forced on Bosnia when the Slovenians and above all the Croatians gave up the fight for a new union: only "Serboslavia" was left. The rise of Serb nationalism hardly made a mini-Yugoslavia dominated by Slobodan Milosevic appealing. The referendum on independence demanded by the "international community" was boobytrapped, given the lack of any consensus on how people would live together in this "independent" country that would be so dependent on its closest neighbors. The great majority of the Serb community abstained in droves out of concern at finding itself a minority outside a Yugoslav framework. And Radovan Karadzic's Serb militias began dismembering Bosnia.

The Greater Serbia policy, imposed in the name of Serb self-determination, was planned and carried out according to a project charted cynically on maps. Vojislav Seselj had been jailed in the 1980s for drawing such maps. In order to take the plans off paper and implement them on the ground, three things were needed: the right *context* and the required *military and political means*.

The *context* was the crisis of the late 1980s and the rise of nationalist governments, along with the fears spread among people by the crisis and the uncertainties that it gave rise to.

The *military means* were supplied by the alliance described earlier between the Serbian government, the now-pro-Serb Yugoslav army, and the paramilitary far right groups with their Chetnik traditions.

But the *political means* were forged through summit-level agreements made well before the war between leaders of the Serbian and Croatian republics, each determined to build "their" country and "settle" the conflicts between them by dismembering Bosnia-Herzegovina. Their hands were strengthened by the policies of the so-called "international community" and by the absence of any credible alternative.

## THE PURGE OF BOSNIA-HERZEGOVINA TARGETS THE MUSLIMS

Serb nationalism and Croat nationalism (after Serb nationalism had tried to incorporate Bosnia-Herzegovina in the Serbian-Montenegrin federation and Croat nationalism had tried to incorporate it in Croatia) had a common interest inherent in their common logic: denying and suffocating the real, ethnically mixed Bosnia, and isolating and disenfranchising its Muslim component. The Muslim community's resistance impeded a total partition of Bosnia-Herzegovina on the model of 1939.[15] But Bosnia had to be reduced to the smallest possible size. The Serbian-Croatian alliance set about it with a hypocritical combination of means. In this fight, Muslim nationalism and the opposition parties' weakness would disarm the Bosnian cause.

The military and paramilitary dimension of Bosnia-Herzegovina's dismemberment were essential. On the Serb side there was a plan worked out in advance, known by its code name "RAM," developed by 1991. The plan emanated from the Yugoslav army, which was experiencing major internal divisions at the time. This is what Xavier Bougarel says about them:

> This army was still divided between a Greater Serbian current, which openly backed the [Serb nationalist party] SDS and its militias, and

a Titoist current, which was tempted to view Bosnia-Herzegovina as a last refuge in case of a confrontation with Milosevic.... The "RAM" plan, anticipating stage-managed interethnic incidents and the occupation of strategic points by the federal army, relied mainly on the SDS militias recruited among the Serb population of Bosnia-Herzegovina.[16]

Zeljko Raznjatovic's ("Arkan") and Vojislav Seselj's militias, which came from Serbia and "supervised" the main crimes of ethnic cleansing, also worked together with Karadzic's SDS (Serb Democratic Party) militias.

On the Croat side there was also the direct intervention of the official Croatian army, which had been armed very quickly despite the embargo. It was led by Defense Minister Gojko Susak, an advocate of partitioning Bosnia between Croatia and Serbia. It supported the organization of the HVO militias (Croat Defense Council, linked to Tudjman's HDZ [Croat Democratic Community] party). The HVO sometimes fought and sometimes allied with the HOS militias of the Croatian Party of Right, which explicitly claimed the Ustashe heritage. But Tudjman's policy was to integrate the militias quickly into the official armed forces, to try to control them. The Party of Right in fact opposed Tudjman on the issue of partitioning Bosnia. Its line was still more Greater Croatian: it aimed at incorporating all of Bosnia into Croatia.

Among these militias (Serb or Croat) a large proportion were common-law criminals, who literally fed on war.

As for the Bosnian government, it did not prepare for the war in any way. President Izetbegovic seems to have been convinced that there would not be any war in Bosnia, and that in any case the officers of the Yugoslav army (or at least some of them) would defend Bosnia-Herzegovina's integrity. That was a fatal underestimation of the fact that 60 percent of the officers were Serbs, mainly from areas of Bosnia-Herzegovina where many of the Ustashe's massacres of Serbs took place during World War II. This is why, when the Yugoslav army withdrew from Bosnia at the Security Council's request on May 19, 1992, many officers of Bosnian origin (including General Mladic) stayed (and held on to most of the heavy equipment). Nevertheless a good number of former Yugoslav army officers (including both Serbs and Croats) deserted and accepted positions in the army loyal to Bosnia-Herzegovina's government.

Despite Croatia's formal recognition of Bosnian independence, the Croat HVO refused to be integrated into the Bosnian army in most areas of the country. As early as 1992 the HVO carried out a policy hostile to the Muslim community and Bosnian army in central Bosnia and the Mostar area. The Bosnia army thus had to be created from scratch during the war, fighting in fact on two fronts. At the beginning it relied on scattered initiatives, in which real, war-profiteering bandits were swept up in its ranks as well. The Bosnian government exerted itself to professionalize this army: first by subjecting the militias to central discipline, then by carrying out purges.

The war in Bosnia was for a long time presented mainly in the light of the Serbian aggression, which was the most direct and in the beginning the most visible and violent. From this standpoint, the breaking off of the Muslim-Croat alliance in spring 1993 appeared as a surprise or a betrayal, a result of the Serbs' "bad example" insidiously influencing the "Croat democrats." (This was the theory of "infection.") Such an interpretation can be upheld only by ignoring the Croatian regime's nature and domestic policies, and by overlooking major aspects of the Bosnian crisis from the first days of the war on. For one thing, all three nationalist parties backed projects for Bosnia's "ethnic cantonization" at the start of the negotiations. In addition, while Chetnik forces were laying siege to the cities and cleaning out their "ethnic corridors," the Croat "republic of Herceg-Bosna" was being built: a clear sign of the outlook of the "Herzegovinians" backed by Franjo Tudjman and his minister of defense, Gojko Susak. Here is what the August 1992 Helsinki Watch report said:

> On May 6, 1992, Mate Boban and Radovan Karadzic ... met in Austria, in Graz. Boban and Karadzic are seen respectively as the puppets of Tudjman and Milosevic, and it is generally agreed that the meeting was organized by the presidents of Serbia and Croatia in order to follow up their discussions on partitioning Bosnia-Herzegovina....

> On July 3, 1992, Mate Boban declared the creation in Bosnia-Herzegovina of a quasi-independent Croat state made up of a third of Bosnian territory, free of Serb forces.... This largely Croat region also includes towns and villages where the Muslim community and Serbs are in the majority.... The proclamation of a Croat state in Bosnia had been preceded by pressures brought to bear by Tudjman

on Bosnian President Izetbegovic, aimed at making him agree to form a confederation with Croatia. Faced with President Izetbegovic's resistance, Boban presented him with a virtual ultimatum: either Izetbegovic would proclaim the confederation, or Croat forces stationed near Sarajevo would not come to the city's defense. Boban increased the pressure on the Bosnian government in June and July, by blocking the delivery of weapons that the Sarajevo government had secretly bought....[17]

All this could have been confirmed by anyone who wanted to see what was in front of them, just by traveling to Sarajevo along the "Croat road" through Mostar. Months before the offensive against the Muslim community launched by the Croat HVO in the spring of 1993, Herceg-Bosna functioned as a state within the state. It had its own currency, its own flag, and its Croat militias, which wore uniforms still indiscreetly displaying the German flag. Sarajevo remained under siege for political reasons, not military reasons. In Stup near Sarajevo, Croat and Serb militias were hobnobbing while shells were raining on the city.

The Croat HDZ party linked to Tudjman formally stood for Bosnia-Herzegovina's independence and territorial integrity. But as early as November 1991 it formed two autonomous Croat regions: Posavina in northern Bosnia, and "Herceg-Bosna" in eastern Herzegovina and central Bosnia. The HDZ also purged its "Bosnian" wing as early as February 1992 to the benefit of Mate Boban, who appeared in public at Tudjman's side. Stjepan Kljujic, considered by all the Bosnians as one of their own, was not only pushed out of Boban's HDZ but also out of the Bosnian collective presidency at the time. Furthermore, the Croat members of this presidency (which consisted at the time of two Muslims, two Serbs, two Croats, and a "Yugoslav") were in fact installed in Zagreb for the duration of the war, until the March 1994 Washington agreement established a new Muslim-Croat federation. They paid their allegiance directly to Tudjman's policies and hastened to sign the plans for the ethnic carve-up of Bosnia.

Shortly after Kljujic was pushed aside, in fact, the HDZ asked the Badinter Commission to rephrase the referendum on self-determination. It wanted an explicit mention of the existence of "constituent and sovereign nations organized on their national lands (cantons)."[18] This phraseology emphasized giving territorial form to ethnicity and nationality and on guaranteeing the three "sovereign nations" the right to self-determination (i.e., separation). At the time the Muslim SDA (Party for Democratic Action) objected, insisting for its part on Bosnia's sovereignty and unity. Behind all the conjunctural alliances, this remains a profound source of disagreement right up to the present.

Even inside the formal framework of the second Croatian-Bosnian alliance (beginning in March 1994), there have still been several dynamics at work. Even if internal and international political pressures (particularly from the United States) have brought about a change in official Croatian policy, the threat of Greater or "Medium-Greater" Croatia remains. President Tudjman is well known to prefer a logic of ethnic partition of Bosnia in alliance with the Serbs to a Croat-Muslim federation. In January 1995, after Jimmy Carter's mission, the contact group's "peace plan" was considered nonnegotiable (on the basic question of a unitary Bosnia); but the Croat spokesperson (though a member of the Bosnian government) agreed with Radovan Karadzic that the plan could still be discussed.

The alliances at the top between Milosevic and Tudjman and between Bosnian Serb and Croat warlords and militias caught the Muslim community—and more generally those who assumed they were "Bosnians," the "impure" urban population—in a terrible trap.[19] It allowed Bosnian Serb warlord Radovan Karadzic to sit at the negotiating table, legitimized by Mate Boban, head of Croat Herceg-Bosna. This alliance combined with Croat pressures on their Muslim "allies" to ensure that the mixed "Bosnian" reality would not be represented in the negotiations: so President Izetbegovic speaks for the "Muslim side." But why did he accept this, if not because of his own ambiguous choices? And why could Boban force his way in, if not because he "betrayed" the Bosnian cause from the very beginning?

Like Tudjman, Boban was playing two games at the same time. He allied with the Muslim community against the Serb enemy, which was allowed to assault Sarajevo (though the "allied" Croat and Bosnian military forces could have relieved the city) in hopes of a foreign intervention against the Serbs; at the same time he allied with the Serb enemy in a project for carving up Bosnia-Herzegovina, which was negotiated by Milosevic and Tudjman well before the war broke out. Boban's and Tudjman's "help" took on the form of permanent blackmail, in which the hundreds of thousands of Muslim refugees in Croatia served as hostages.

### Muslim nationalism serves the Bosnian cause — badly

Muslim nationalism would weaken the Bosnian cause. True, Muslim nationalism was moderate. It alone of the nationalist movements at least officially defended a multiethnic Bosnia-Herzegovina. The reasons for its position are historical and pragmatic. First of all, Serb or Croat nationalism in Bosnia can each turn toward another country and try to enlarge it at Bosnia's expense; but there is no "great hinterland" for the Bosnian Muslim community. Bosnia is the only country they have. Even there they have only a relative majority—all the more precarious if one goes by strict religious affiliation.

It is thus in the Muslim community's interest more than any other's to maintain a multiethnic Bosnia, because a multiethnic Bosnia is necessary for the Muslim community's existence. This reality explains why nonethnic parties won so many votes in urban Muslim communities. It also undoubtedly pushes "Muslim nationalism" toward compromises and alliances. But what kind of compromises and alliances—and to create what kind of country?

The SDA (Alija Izetbegovic's Muslim party) is the bearer of two main dynamics. Its *religious component* is committed not so much to Bosnia as to a Muslim state. But Bosnia is far from having even a potential Islamic majority. Izetbegovic's wavering in response to proposals to cantonize or break up Bosnia (including his willingness as late as early 1995 to renegotiate the contact group proposal) are doubtless due to the fact that two different approaches are available to this current: on the one hand, a "Muslim state" sliced off from Bosnia that could likely be more easily islamicized; or defense of Muslim interests within a united Bosnia.

The second approach has been favored from the beginning, given that slicing off a "Muslim state" from this ethnically mixed land would be a tragic dead end. But the difficulty of keeping Bosnia alive by means of either an agreement or military victory makes Izetbegovic incline periodically toward signing a proposal for three-way partition.

Within this current there definitely exist moderate strains (which Izetbegovic embodies: the whole of his political pragmatism pushes him simultaneously toward the West and the Arab countries); but other strains, more fundamentalist, can only grow in a war whose main victims are Muslims. The fundamentalists look to Islamic regimes abroad for their main support—but where else can they get support?

The SDA's second main component (generally associated with current prime minister Haris Silajdzic) is more *secular*. It is certainly no more homogeneous than the other current. A good number of ex-Communists have joined it: Fikret Abdic, chief executive officer of Agrokomerk, belonged to it before he was expelled when he declared the autonomy of his province in the Bihac enclave. This secular wing of the SDA may give expression to a Bosnian nationalist current that wants to consolidate the Bosnian state and its frontiers in the interests of the Muslim ethnic-national community (*Bosnjiaci*). Bosnian government policy is undoubtedly often a compromise between different currents—and the shifting alliances that the government concludes.

The SDA's official "multiethnic" rhetoric in this framework has taken two forms, one reflecting a search for alliances among the so-called "citizen" (non-nationalist) parties, the other by contrast reflecting a search for allies among the nationalist parties.

The first form, predominating at the beginning of the war and aiming at the "international community's" support, is a project for a *unitary country of citizens*. This is also the orientation of the antinationalist opposition. But this first variant—a "unitary" country—while perhaps popular in the ethnically mixed cities, quickly evokes suspicion from a large proportion of the Serb and Croat *minority* populations in Bosnia (just as a unitary Yugoslavia was rejected by all the minority communities, though easily accepted by the Serb majority that was not afraid of being discriminated against behind a façade of equality). In the Balkan context, affirming citizenship, without any guarantee (or experience) of equal political, socioeconomic, and cultural treatment for different peoples, fails to address many important (social, cultural, and political) concerns.

Second, there is the contrasting project of building a *country of three nations* (in fact two nations in the case of the Croat-Muslim alliance, which makes Serb residents of the federation second-class citizens). According to the nationalist conception, this orientation means rejecting the emergence of a mixed citizenship. It aims instead at tight control through "ethnic cantons." It leads to a permanent struggle to win new local majorities and new territories. It substitutes a division of power on an exclusively ethnic and national basis for any confrontation between political programs. While the Bosnian presidency affirms its secularism and multiethnic content, it has most often appeared in public—under the leadership of Alija Izetbegovic, who represents a religious current—to be "Muslim." Izetbegovic in fact mixes religious ceremony with his official presidential activities.

The cabinet did initially include ministers from the non-nationalist opposition. But power was at that time largely concentrated in the hands of a presidency whose "entire strategy depended on the internationalization of the Bosnian conflict."[20] It did not really publicize and defend the "platform of the Bosnian collective presidency" adopted in June 1992,[21] whose orientation was inconsistent with the Croat-Muslim alliance. This platform was at once a political appeal to all the Bosnian communities and a constitutional draft that rejected both ethnic carve-up and a unitarist approach. Publicizing the platform was all the more important because the "Islamic Declaration" written by Izetbegovic in 1970 had declared for an Islamic state as soon as Muslims secured a majority.[22]

This declaration came to be widely published and distributed in the 1990s. It was used in Belgrade and Zagreb (where they were quite willing to confuse the 1970 date of composition with the 1990 date of publication) in order to convince people abroad, but also among the Serb and Croat populations, that "Bosnian = Muslim = fundamentalist." The hypocrisy of this propaganda is clear. Fundamentalism was less of a threat in the Bosnian Muslim community, a majority of whom are secularized and opposed to a religious state, than almost anywhere one can imagine.[23] Izetbegovic was doubtless a victim of rival nationalist policies.

But Izetbegovic was also less well situated than others in the Muslim community to speak in the name of *all* the communities against building ethnically based countries. Fikret Abdic, for example, a nonreligious Muslim leader in the Bihac area, had won more votes than Izetbegovic and was popular among Serbs and Croats. Might Abdic have done better than Izetbegovic as president?

### *The Bihac enclave: the "Republic of Agrokomerk"*

Fikret Abdic is chief executive officer of a conglomerate, Agrokomerk, which went bankrupt in August 1987 in the wake of a political and financial scandal. At the time Abdic was a member of the central committee of the League of Yugoslav Communists. He decided to support Izetbegovic's party, the SDA, in the November 1990 elections, though without sharing all of Izetbegovic's religious convictions. Very popular locally, he won more votes than Izetbegovic.

But more a businessman than a politician, Abdic decided to leave the presidency to Izetbegovic in order to focus his attention on Agrokomerk in Velika-Kladusa in the Bihac enclave in northwestern Bosnia-Herzegovina. The company flourished thanks to its good relations with the neighboring Serbs and Croats and its offices in Croatia and Vienna. It was the foundation of Abdic's power in the Muslim-majority Bihac enclave, which was part of the "republic" assigned to the Muslim community in the framework of the Owen-Stoltenberg plan (and was one of the UN's so-called "safe havens").

Abdic was a member of the Bosnian collective presidency until his expulsion in October 1993, when he proclaimed his region "the Autonomous Province of Western Bosnia." The secession was doubtless motivated by pragmatism, as a glance at the map makes understandable: the Bihac enclave is cut off from "its (Muslim) country" and surrounded by Serb- and Croat-controlled areas. But the secession also undoubtedly expresses a judgment made by many of the long-secularized Muslims who made up the great majority of the Muslim community: the creation of a "Muslim republic," caught between hostile Serb and Croat forces, in which radical Islamic currents would gain strength, could well be a tragic dead end for the Muslim community itself. Was Abdic not so much "betraying the Bosnian cause" as defending it in his own way?

This question was answered dramatically in August 1994, when the secession provoked an offensive against Abdic's forces by the Bosnian army's Fifth Corps. When the Bosnian army continued its offensive against the Serbs, Abdic and his forces reacted by coming to the aid of the Serb militias. He will be a "joker" for Radovan Karadzic in the negotiations under way. Rather than resorting to ethnic cleansing of this overwhelmingly Muslim area, the Serb forces probably aim above all at making the Fifth Corps disband or withdraw. They will try to negotiate a Bosnian retreat while consolidating Abdic's power in his fief.

## *A counterproductive alliance*

Rather than appealing to the Bosnian peoples and winning their confidence, Izetbegovic relied on his legal majority in the referendum on independence, which had secured the "international community's" recognition of independent Bosnia. No doubt he hoped that the "international community" would save Bosnia by intervening militarily. This led Bosnian propogandists to reduce the war to a one-dimensional foreign (Serbian) aggression, ignoring its other aspects and the depth of the conflicts inside Bosnia-Herzegovina itself.

The first Croat-Muslim alliance (which fell apart in the spring of 1993) exacerbated this logic, wrapping Herceg-Bosna and the Croat pressures in a veil of silence and directing all attacks at the "single, Serbo-Communist aggressor." Tariq Haveric, one of the leaders of the Liberal Party of Bosnia-Herzegovina, now an immigrant in Paris, has denounced "the illusion of a 'natural alliance between Croats and Muslims' in the struggle against the Serbs."[24] This alliance was bound to transform Serb fears into full-fledged paranoia.

The extremist militias and the media controlled by nationalist governments had manipulated memories of past genocide in order to evoke fears that gave the Greater Serbia project its popular base. It is logical that this project took root particularly among the Serbs of Croatia and Bosnia-Herzegovina (i.e., the areas where the Greater Croatian massacres had taken place). The outcomes of the "referendums" organized in these two regions (in favor of unification with Serbia) were doubtless in part the result of the local warlords' terrorism.[25] But they were probably also the result of a chain reaction of fear.

There has been talk in the corridors about conflicts between Izetbegovic and the armed forces under mixed command that predominate in Tuzla: Izetbegovic was said to prefer seeing Sarajevo besieged to seeing it saved by currents that are critical of him. These rumors cannot be confirmed.[26] But their substance is plausible. Bogdan Useljenicki speaks openly of two opposed logics within the "Bosnian" armed forces: "it was no longer timely ... to praise the multinational or antifascist character of the Bosnian army; the time had come for its most homogeneous, most reislamicized and ... most bloodthirsty units."[27] Tariq Haveric, leader of the Bosnian Liberal Party, also criticizes the Bosnian army's orientation in central Bosnia during its spring 1993 offensive: "instead of eliminating the HVO as a military factor and doing everything to protect Croat civilians, certain Bosnian units carried out 'ethnic cleansing' operations themselves in central Bosnia."[28]

Defending the multiethnic Bosnian cause requires us to discuss the Islamic currents that actually exist, which will target "bad Muslims" as their first victims and facilitate Greater Serbian and Greater Croatian policies. It is still necessary to distinguish the defensive violence of those who resist ethnic cleansing from the violence of the aggressors. But ends and means must be consistent with one another. Because some of the Muslims in the SDA aim at building an Islamic state, Croat and Serb civilians are often not distinguished from their leaders and nationalist militias. This is something more than a simple response by victims to outside aggression.

### The multiethnic resistance

Resistance by those who said they were Bosnian rather than Muslim, Serb, or Croat was concentrated partly in Sarajevo and more clearly in the Tuzla region.[29] But evidently the predominant non-nationalist orientation in Tuzla could only be weakened by the Croat-Muslim alliance and the policies carried out in Sarajevo. Tuzla's non-nationalists were also squeezed by masses of refugees fleeing from regions "cleansed" by Serb militiamen: the refugees were more open to Muslim extremist positions.

It was certainly difficult for non-nationalist Bosnians to find spokespeople who will publicly defend an alternative to the Bosnian government's approach. Very much constrained by the siege of their cities and their lack of weapons,[30] currents favorable to multicultural mixing were in addition divided among themselves. Some of them had chosen to join the first government and support President Izetbegovic; as Bogdan Useljenicki suggests, "these parties are willing to legitimize the government of Alija Izetbegovic and his entourage and keep quiet about his ambiguous policies" in "the hope of a foreign military intervention."[31] In order to secure this support, Izetbegovic has stuck despite everything to a secular rhetoric that advocates a multiethnic Bosnia-Herzegovina.

Understandably, the extremely weak non-nationalist parties could see no alternative to supporting Izetbegovic. But has this perhaps contributed to "stifling Tuzla," the symbol of an alternative resistance? And were liberal responses and proposals for a "state of citizens" enough to counteract the dismemberment of the crisis-laden Bosnian "mini-Yugoslavia" by the same segregationist logic that had earlier pulled apart the larger Yugoslavia? How can these questions not be asked at the moment when the mixed "Bosnian" civilization is closer to death than ever before, and still worthy of being defended?

## FROM THE VANCE-OWEN PLAN TO THE CROAT-MUSLIM FEDERATION

The first proposals for Bosnia-Herzegovina's "cantonization," put forward in March 1992 (see pp. 116-17, below), were quickly challenged by the "Muslim" delegation. The Vance-Owen plan, presented in January 1993, was ambiguously formulated and open to two different readings. In effect, on the one hand, it largely ratified the ethnic partition of Bosnia-Herzegovina sought by Serb and Croat nationalists. But on the other hand, it reaffirmed the integrity of the Bosnian state, with equality among the communities. The ambiguity resided entirely in the true nature of the ten "provinces" envisaged by the plan: what would be their relationships with the Bosnian, Serbian, and Croatian states?

The draft plan was immediately signed by Mate Boban for the Croats. It was described by the Croatian newspaper *Globus* (on January 8, 1993) as "the greatest Croat political triumph of the twentieth century": the plan made possible the effective establishment of a minimalist version of Greater Croatia. In fact it implicitly ratified the "Republic of Herceg-Bosna" that was proclaimed in Herzegovina as early as the summer of 1992. The plan largely included the territory claimed by Herceg-Bosna in provinces assigned to the Croats—with more than 25 percent of Bosnia's land for a Croat population that made up 18 percent of Bosnia-Herzegovina's total.

Formally however, the plan the Croats signed did not recognize the existence of "republics." The Bosnian government was pushed by the international negotiators to sign the draft on the basis of a favorable reading of it, which would preserve the Bosnian republic's integrity. In the end it did so.

No sooner was the signature dry than the Croat HVO (the military organization linked to the HDZ, Tudjman's and Boban's party) could claim to be "applying the plan" when they demanded the withdrawal of Muslim forces from the "Croat provinces" and launched an offensive against the Muslim community of Mostar; and the Muslim community could on the contrary reproach their former allies with "not applying the plan." That was the beginning of the open conflict between the HVO and the Bosnian government, which lasted until spring 1994.

Did this plan "protect" the fiction of a Bosnian state any better against Greater Serbian projects than against Greater Croatian projects?

The plan "granted" the Bosnian Serbs, more scattered and much more mixed in with the other communities, Serb majority provinces that were neither connected to one another nor bordering on Serbia the way that Herceg-Bosna bordered on Croatia. This was why Bosnian Serbs rejected the plan in their "referendum." And this was the logic of the "cleansing" of "ethnic corridors," where the violence was all the worse because Serbs were in a minority.

The ambiguities of the Vance-Owen plan soon made way for the international negotiators' official acceptance of the division of Bosnia-Herzegovina into "three states" along ethnic lines. This new "principle" was made explicit in the Owen-Stoltenberg plan after the August 1993 Washington meeting, which brought together representatives of the United States, European Economic Community, and Russia.

The practical result of this "peace plan" has been the generalization of battle fronts in Bosnia-Herzegovina, with 2.7 million displaced persons and refugees. In 1994 there were 3.5 million displaced persons and refugees on ex-Yugoslav territory and 750,000 asylum seekers outside it.[32]

Contrary to what the negotiators expected, the Serbian-Croatian plan supported by Owen and Stoltenberg has produced large-scale instability for all the concerned countries and communities.

First, the logic of ethnic partition has encouraged each side to wage permanent war in order to try to make unviable countries viable: establish "ethnic corridors," gain access to the sea, win more land in order to be able to settle on it the hundreds of thousands of refugees that exist in each community.

Second, ethnic cleansing will be carried out everywhere all the more eagerly once it is accepted as a basis for forming countries. Despite the massacres and the refugees, no region is homogeneous. There will be a myriad of new oppressed minorities and a tendency toward endless fragmentation of existing countries.

The first sacrificial victims are the Bosnians who still want to live together, and in particular the Muslim community that has no other country besides Bosnia-Herzegovina. We can understand when they try to enlarge the "Indian reservations" that have been generously assigned to them. But no single community has won out through such policies. "Bad Serbs," "bad Croats," and "bad Muslims" have fled abroad; there has been economic catastrophe and "brain drain"; the young are deserting. More old people are commiting suicide every day in Serbia. Each political "camp" is disintegrating: this is perhaps the only hope for pluralism, but without the redefinition of a common project, nothing will be able to stop the disintegration.

### *The Croat-Muslim federation: a peaceful alternative?*

"*Budi svoj* (be yourself)." We can borrow this motto from the conclusion of Midhat Begic's essay, "The Muslim Writer in Yugoslav Literature."[33] Like today,

> Muslim writers before 1914 saw themselves driven to choose between two nationalities, Serb or Croat, while young intellectuals asked themselves more and more where a path could be found that would lead to human dignity.

Was the second Croat-Muslim alliance, to a certain extent forced on them by the White House (after the failure of the meetings between Tudjman and Izetbegovic), aimed at forming a counterweight to Russo-Serb alliances in the Balkans? We are seeing the reestablishment, once more behind the backs of the peoples involved, of old-time "spheres of influence." But even if the might of the "great powers" demands vigilance, nothing is inevitable: the Croat-Muslim union will be in any event what the protagonists on the ground make it. It is initially open to several different variants.

The conflictual détente between Croats and Muslims took place in conditions more favorable to the Muslim community than the 1992 alliance, which died in the spring of 1993 with the ethnic cleansing of Mostar. The "Muslim" side is more alert to its allies' doubletalk. The Bosnian army has been substantially strengthened and professionalized. At the end of 1993 and beginning of 1994 it retook almost half of the land conquered by the Croat HVO in central Bosnia. Croat military defeats have led to a new, critical consciousness, not only among some Bosnian Croats but in Croatia and within the Catholic Church. Interventions in the war by the Croatian army have evoked threats of sanctions from the "international community."

Pressures in favor of the new alliance have thus come from inside as well as outside Bosnia. The split from Tudjman's HDZ party in early

1994 by prominent members of his regime such as Stipe Mesic (the last president of the old Yugoslav federation) was provoked in particular by Tudjman's and Mate Boban's Bosnian policy, explicitly criticized as an aggression against Bosnia-Herzegovina. The creation of a Bosnian Croat "Consultative Council" also made it easier to push (Herceg-Bosna leader) Boban aside, and eventually bring Stjepan Kljujic back into the Bosnian presidency at the head of a new Croat political formation.

Pressure from Washington for a new Croat-Muslim alliance was thus preceded (and transmitted) by something of a Croat opposition. Each of the two sides had an interest in signing the March 1994 Washington agreement, which set up the new Croat-Muslim federation and proposed a confederation with neighboring Croatia. Each of the two communities gained some more breathing room; a "Muslim" state made up of a few unviable enclaves without access to the sea willingly made way for a more viable federation; and the Croat HDZ, while keeping Herceg-Bosna hidden up its sleeve, gained high positions within the federation, and above all could be happy (moreso than the Muslim community) at the prospect of confederation with Croatia. But the accords were signed by the Muslim SDA and Croat HDZ, i.e., nationalist parties whose basic orientations are still antagonistic. The constitution was (and is) weighed down by conflicting interpretations and implementations.[34] The federation's establishment went together with a ceasefire (fragile—but how precious for the people at risk!) between the Croat militias and the Bosnian army. This undermined Islamic fundamentalist propaganda that portrayed the war as the Christians' war against the Muslims. There also have appeared some signs of easing of the crisis, notably an alternative to an ethnic partition of Bosnia-Herzegovina. The growth of "civic" initiatives bears witness to it. Along with the creation of the Croat Consultative Council, about 500 Bosnian Serbs, representing the roughly 150,000 Serbs still living in "Muslim" territory, met in Sarajevo in March 1994 (with Russian and U.S. envoys in attendance). They declared their commitment to multiethnic Bosnia, their refusal to let Radovan Karadzic represent all the Bosnian Serbs, and their rejection of any policy of ethnic cleansing. They set up a "Serb Consultative Council," asking (in vain) to be represented in all the negotiations.

In the spring of 1994, on the eve of the Serb offensive against the Gorazde enclave, each nationalist party was thus experiencing major internal differences and conflicts. We have noted among the Croats the HDZ's crisis after Mate Boban's fall and the Catholic Church's attempt to distance itself from the Croatian regime (confirmed during the pope's September 1994 visit to Zagreb by a speech that Croat nationalists thought was "too internationalist"). In the Muslim SDA, the differences mentioned above grew worse when Fikret Abdic spoke out demanding an end to the war and declaring his Velika Kladusa fief in the Bihac enclave "an autonomous province of Bosnia." Among the Serbs, finally, the public divorce between Milosevic and the Serbian far right (unfortunately still backed by the Orthodox Church) already went together with a visible attempt to dissociate himself from "Serb cousins" in neighboring republics—in hopes of getting the sanctions lifted.

So in the spring of 1994 the establishment of the Muslim-Croat federation seemed to sidetrack completely the European "peace plans" for partitioning Bosnia-Herzegovina, and to encourage political differentiation.

The offensive by General Mladic's Serb troops against the Gorazde enclave (one of the UN-declared "safe havens") took place in this context. Making nonsense of NATO ultimatums and UN commitments, it highlighted international divergences, which the powers tried to solve by setting up the "contact group" (with representatives of the United States, Russia, France, Britain, and Germany).

Meanwhile nationalist dynamics remained at work within the Muslim-Croat federation. In addition the Serb Civic Council had raised in Sarajevo the crucial issue of Serbs' place in the new federation. An amendment was submitted to the draft constitution, proposing to grant the Serb people the same status as the two others. It was tabled. In early 1995 it had still not been adopted.

How could the 150,000 Serbs within the federation be won to the project, and how could the Serbs within the "Serb Republic of Bosnia" be won away from Greater Serbia, without equal status for all the Bosnian peoples, without a *political offensive* that would weaken Radovan Karadzic? In the absence of such an offensive, the federation boiled down to an anti-Serb alliance between Muslim and Croat nationalisms, each of them exclusionary, each of them trying to control "its" cantons and bits of power.

The main point of the federation became then a military one: enabling the Bosnian army to launch "national liberation" offensives as the Bosnian generals called them, in hopes of retaking the territory occupied by Karadzic's forces.

The "peace plans" proposed by the contact group were no more than a replay of the proposals to divide Bosnia-Herzegovina into three states—or hypothetically two, 51 percent for the federation and 49 percent for the Serbs. In reality no one accepted this. Karadzic's Serb forces explicitly demanded recognition of their republic, its territorial coherence, and its right to link up with Serbia as the Muslim-Croat federation would link up with Croatia. The Bosnian leaders for their part did not accept the break-up of Bosnia, which would seal an outside aggression. They prepared their offensives. But they took advantage of the Serb rejection of the plan, accepting it formally as it stood—but without any renegotiation.

The offensive of the Bosnian army's Fifth Corps during the summer of 1994 led to a dramatic turning point. First fighting against Fikret Abdic's secessionist forces which they put to flight, the Bosnian army then attacked the Serb forces. After a tactical withdrawal, the Serb counteroffensive, victorious in the so-called Bihac "safe haven," relied by the end of 1994 on the Serbs of the Croatian Krajina and on Abdic and his followers, now open Serb allies. Whatever speeches were made in Zagreb, no effective support for the Bosnian forces was forthcoming from Croatia. Negotiations were thus to resume in early 1995 against a backdrop of tensions within the Croat-Muslim alliance and victories by the extremist wings of Serb nationalism.

Confederal links between Croatia, Serbia and a multinational Bosnia recognized by its neighbors could contribute to rapprochement between Bosnia's different communities. But a merger between the "Serb Republic of Bosnia" and neighboring Serbia—as advocated by French minister Alain Juppé in early 1995—would almost certainly mean the consummation of Bosnia's break-up, with the break-up of the Croat-Muslim federation as its first step: the Serbs' situation within the federation would become increasingly intolerable. A victory of Karadzic's line would also fuel symmetrical demands by Croat nationalism. Far from leading to peace, this plan would exacerbate Serb-Croat tensions in Croatia over the Krajina issue and generally result in a hardening among the most extremist currents in each community. Minorities would be more trapped than ever inside each "ethnic territory." Refugees' right to return would be ruled out. Refugee issues would plague ex-Yugoslavia—and Europe—for years.

This would seem to justify people like Yves Lacoste who had said for months that a point of no return had been reached, and that the best thing left to do is organize "population transfers."[35] Journalist Jacques Merlino has also been calling for "realism,"[36] relying on the words of the French ambassador to Bosnia:

> It is completely legitimate to dream of a Bosnia whose inhabitants would feel themselves Bosnian first and Croats, Serbs, or Muslims second. What is not legitimate is to reason as if Mr. Izetbegovic's Bosnia was ever capable of realizing this dream. And what is frankly irresponsible is to claim to base a policy on this dream, calling on the international community in general and France in particular to realize this dream by force if necessary.[37]

It is true that not all the inhabitants of Bosnia-Herzegovina have felt themselves "Bosnian" first and Serbs, Croats, or Muslims second. It is just as true that the arrival of "ethnic" parties in power in Bosnia opened the era of dismemberment: the "international community" cannot resolve the Bosnian crisis in place of the communities involved. But the Bosnian blend is not a dream—no one wages war against a dream.

"Peace" plans built on exclusion have relied on the warlords and nationalist parties, not on those who have resisted them and still resist them. That has been the "frankly irresponsible" choice: to have rejected the dream and chosen the nightmare.

# 5

# The "International Community" on Trial

What is the role of "outside factors" in the dismantling of Yugoslavia? We will not do a systematic study, but only indicate the factors that seem most important.[1]

We have already emphasized the impact of free market economic policies in fostering Yugoslavia's disintegration—though the dead ends and monstrosities of "existing socialism" and the apparent building of a new Europe around the 1991 Maastricht treaty made this harder to see at the beginning of the 1990s, above all for Yugoslav democrats. These two points—the evaluation of "really existing socialism," and projects for building the European Union—both deserve analysis at length, since it is absolutely true that socialism was identified with bureaucratic planning and democracy was identified with the market.[2]

Broad currents in the Western left upheld Yugoslav self-management as a third way. For our part we have analyzed it as a contradictory experience based on a partial break with Stalinism.[3] It suffered in addition from its isolation in a doubly hostile environment. Whatever rapprochements there were with the Soviet big brother on the one side and whatever insertion into the capitalist world on the other, there was only a balance of tensions, never international relations that were propitious for the development of a third way. The attempt to maintain single-party rule while broadening the scope for decentralized economic activity necessarily led to the break-up of the party, the disintegration of socioeconomic links based on solidarity, waste, and a crisis of the system's very identity. In this sense the Yugoslav experience foreshadowed the upheavals in Eastern Europe, the USSR and soon after in China.

The second half of the 1980s witnessed economic recovery in the global North and a deepening gap with the East (and South). On one side of the gap, the bureaucracies of the so-called socialist countries, imprisoned in the political and economic relationships that ensured their rule, sank into crisis or sought to transform themselves into new bourgeoisies without capital. In Yugoslavia, successive economic reforms that maintained or even reinforced the role of the ruling party left a system in their wake that was weakened from within and made more vulnerable to shocks from without. This system was struck full force by the world capitalist crisis. In Yugoslavia as elsewhere, the systematic repression of domestic opposition prevented any experimentation with democratic socialist alternatives.[4]

On the other side of the gap, the technological revolution has shown really existing capitalism's capacity for technological innovation—and the view of capitalism from Eastern Europe was attractive shop windows and the democracy of the developed countries. But *destructive innovation* under capitalism has facilitated attacks on the whole safety net inherited from the traumas of the 1929 depression and the post-World War II relationship of forces: an era in which Keynes said that capitalism would not survive unless it "socialized" itself.

Capitalist globalization in the context of a collapse of solidarity movements could only be barbarous, deeply inegalitarian, and based on the principle of might-makes-right. The visible hand of the International Monetary Fund imposes its management criteria on the South and East—though not on the country with the world's biggest debt, the United States. The GATT negotiations have divided markets among developed capitalist countries that have powerful tools for protecting their economies. What country, what region of the world would not like to join this winners' circle? In order to gain its favor, the "European traditions" of Croatia, Slovenia, the Czech Republic, the Baltic states, and Ukraine have been praised to the skies—*as weapons against other peoples* (Asians, Balkan peoples, and other "barbarians"), so that the most developed areas can cut themselves off from the rest. As if the rest did not also want to be (meaning live as well as) "Europeans" themselves!

The trap is that free market prescriptions, applied in the current conditions in Eastern Europe, bring about deindustrialization and cultural destruction more than they narrow the gap between East and West. The prescriptions deepen these countries' socioeconomic crisis instead of easing it. Therefore they require authoritarian regimes to push them through.

This is the first set of international factors that should be analyzed, since they weigh on ex-Yugoslavia as they do on the other countries that used to be called socialist.

Here we will focus on what has particularly characterized the Yugoslav crisis as such: the "international community's" disastrous *realpolitik*.

We do not subscribe to the theory of an "international plot" hatched by Germany and the Vatican, and systematically propagated by Belgrade, at least in the conflict's early days. Whatever this theory's "rational kernel," it has the major disadvantage of downplaying the internal causes and responsibilities for the fragmentation of Yugoslavia and overestimating (judging poorly) the coherence of "Western interests." But the Western governments' shifting and often cynical *realpolitik* has to say the least poured oil on the fire it was supposed to put out.

## MILITARY ISSUES OR POLITICAL STAKES?

Whatever the visible divergences were and are among Western governments over the Yugoslav crisis, the international context today has nothing to do with that of earlier "Balkan" and world wars.

Of course there are spheres of influence handed down by history, and somewhat different objectives. Thanks to the present political and economic balance of forces, Germany is tending to recover what it lost in World War II. France and Britain, in seeking an agreement between Milosevic and Tudjman, probably meant to limit the extent of German influence. As for the United States, it would like to avoid the creation of a politically united Europe, and wants to keep doors open to Russia and Turkey.

But in the eyes of the powers involved, there are no clashes of interest sufficient to justify involvement in a war (still less with one another). As is often said, there is no oil in Bosnia-Herzegovina. This is the simple truth. Yugoslavia lost its strategic importance with Gorbachevism and the fall of the Berlin Wall. The uncertainties of "post-Communism" have consequences for the kind of regimes that are in power, making the divisions of influence still unstable and the future "enemies" unclear. This is true for Russia—NATO's hesitations about how to deal with Russia bear witness to it, and its hesitations are in proportion to the overwhelming domestic and international issues that threaten the future of Yeltsin's regime. Milosevic's "socialism" too is as dubious as Croatian "democracy." How can the Western governments see clearly whom they should rely on to control the new "order" (disorder) in Central Europe, when even the Europe of the Maastricht Treaty is not stabilized and even NATO's future is unclear?

On the economic level, human and natural resources are of course significant throughout ex-Yugoslavia (as they are further east). Slovenia has the trump cards of its "market economy"; Croatia's Adriatic coast is attractive for foreign capital, which invests more readily in tourism than in industry. But all this amounts to laughably little for capital in search of safe investments. Investors are in even less of a hurry to invest in ex-Yugoslavia than in Hungary or Poland, because of the crisis, the war—and behind the crisis and the war, the general uncertainty about borders and about the governments that are supposed to safeguard property.

Now the war has come to the forefront of Western governments' concerns over ex-Yugoslavia, much as initial expectations of a "rush to the east" by euphoric investors have given way to nervousness about political and ethnic disorders in the ex-USSR (equivalent to several Yugoslavias with nuclear bombs). In this context, governments—the European Economic Community as a whole, France, Germany, and the United States—have taken shifting political positions.

Overall, before the June 1991 declarations of independence, these governments tended to prefer a free market, federal Yugoslavia, which would keep its debt under central management and its nationalisms under control. Once the break-up of Yugoslavia was an accomplished fact, Western governments' positions went in different directions. EC governments' main concern was to seem united when in fact they were not. In early 1992 the issue was whether to support or oppose the German position on recognizing Slovenian and Croatian independence. Similarly since summer 1994, the "contact group" set up with representatives of France, Britain, Russia, Germany, and the United States has been struggling to synthesize its members' divergent views. But what are the differences?

# THE "INTERNATIONAL COMMUNITY" ON TRIAL

The U.S. government looked on contentedly from a distance at first at the Europeans getting bogged down in the first "post-Communist" conflict. Then it swung back and forth between two different groups of policymakers. One group tried to respond to pressures from public opinion, which was shocked by the images of the war on television and by the contrast between intervention in Iraq and abstention in Bosnia. These pressures encouraged this group to adopt an interventionist rhetoric (if not a real interventionist policy). U.S. strategic interests in the Arab and Islamic world in general, and efforts to build up diplomatic ties with Turkey in particular, pushed U.S. policy in the same direction: toward seeming to support the Bosnian Muslim cause and Bosnia's survival as a country.

The other group of U.S. policymakers, marked by the Vietnam syndrome, were relectant to get involved in a faraway, confusing war. The NATO general staffs tended to stress this latter aspect. The White House tried out both approaches for a while. It counted on the Europeans' sticking to their positions, so that it could say regretfully that there was nothing it could do.

The two U.S. standpoints doubtless converged ultimately on one certainty made clear by Clinton: that even the United States has no *direct strategic* interest in Bosnia, certainly not a sufficient interest to justify any risk of having their troops die there. Proposals for air strikes (together with the refusal to send ground troops); proposals to lift the embargo on sending arms to the Bosnian Muslim community; and finally sending experts and weapons to support the Bosnian army—all this enabled Washington to commit itself to the Bosnian cause—without actually commiting itself.

In the last analysis, none of the "great powers" has seen any direct interest in ex-Yugoslavia, except avoiding losing men,[5] avoiding being completely written off in the region (which they are more and more anyway), and avoiding the risk of an unwanted Balkan firestorm. The various governments' attention has turned increasingly to their own problems "at home."

Western governments' policies toward refugees from the war, whose horrors they piously continue to denounce, show the extent of their cynicism. The right of asylum is restricted whenever convenient. Visas are required for fleeing Bosnians. Serb deserters are not recognized as refugees. There is a surplus of guiding "principles" that blur and shift according to the requirements of *realpolitik*.

### Peace Plans

**November 1991**  Badinter Commission formed to advise on recognizing new countries.

**February 1992**  Lisbon meeting proposes cantonization of Bosnia. Bosnian Serbs and Croats accept; President Izetbegovic accepts, then rejects. Referendum on independence under EC pressure. Boycott called by Bosnian Serb leader Karadzic.

**April 1992**  Bosnian independence recognized despite Badinter Commission advice. War begins in Sarajevo.

**January 1993**  *Vance-Owen Plan* proposes dividing Bosnia into ten cantons. Croats and Izetbegovic accept; Karadzic calls Serb referendum.

**Spring 1993**  Croat militias begin open "ethnic cleansing" of "their" cantons. Serb referendum rejects plan.

**May 1993**  Establishment of UN "safe havens."

**August 1993**  *Owen-Stoltenberg Plan* proposes dividing Bosnia into three states: Serb (52 percent), Muslim (30 percent) and Croat (18 percent). Izetbegovic demands access to the sea and guarantees. Croats withdraw from Bosnian government. Bosnian army takes offensive in central Bosnia against former Croat allies.

**November 1993**  New EC peace initiative demands that: Serbs give up 3 to 4 percent of Bosnian territory; Croats give the Muslim state access to the sea; the Muslim community must accept the new plan or lose their humanitarian aid.

**February-March 1994**  *Washington Accords* form a Bosnian Muslim-Croat federation and propose a confederation with Croatia.

**May-August 1994**  New "contact group" (France, Britain, Germany, United States, and Russia) proposes dividing Bosnia between Muslim-Croat federation (52 percent) and Serbs (48 percent). Bosnian federation accepts; Milosevic accepts; Bosnian Serbs demand recognition and right to join Serbia.

**Winter 1994**  Following Bosnian offensive and Serb counter-offensive in the Bihac enclave, France proposes allowing Bosnian Serb confederation with Serbia. Jimmy Carter's mediation leads to four-month ceasefire agreement. Bosnia demands Krajina Serbs' withdrawal from Bihac.

# THE "INTERNATIONAL COMMUNITY" ON TRIAL

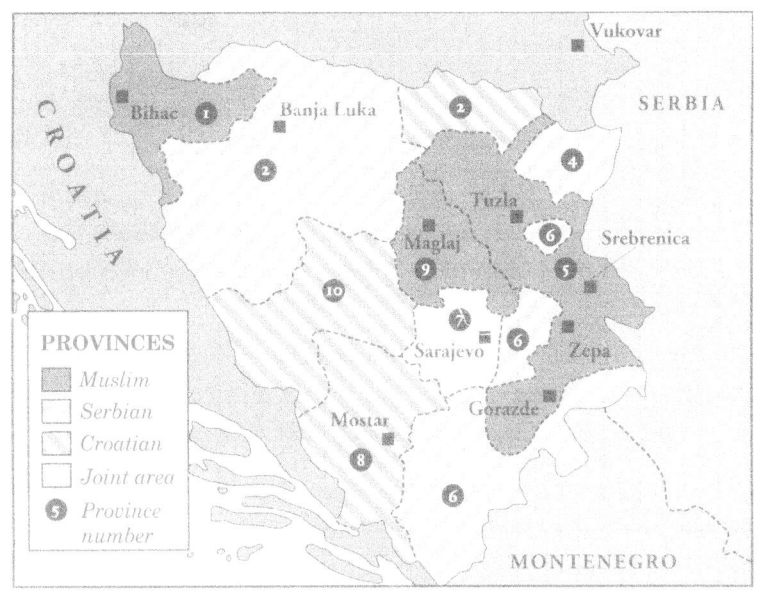

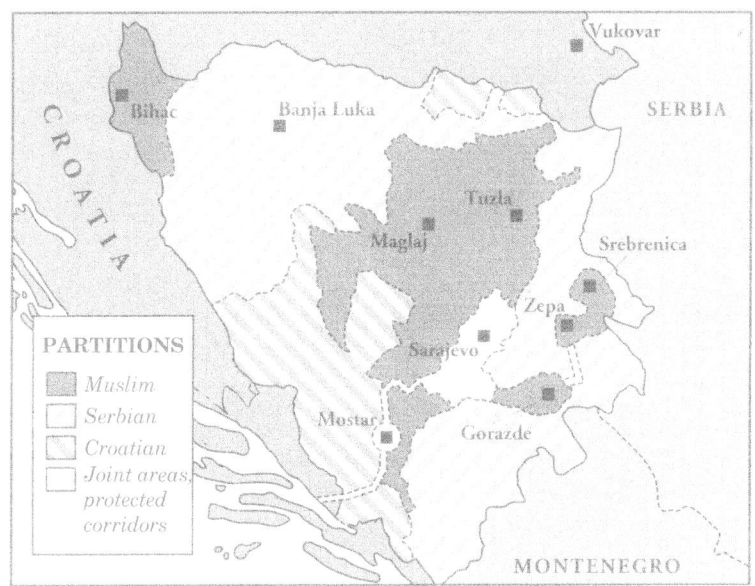

Above: Vance-Owen Plan, January 1993.
Below: Owen-Stoltenberg Plan, August 1993.

Military Fronts, March 1994

# IMMUTABLE FRONTIERS OR RIGHT OF SELF-DETERMINATION?

What is generally called the "international community"—in fact, the main Western governments—has swung back and forth (or has been divided) between two main, conflicting approaches to dealing with the Yugoslav crisis.

The first approach gave priority in practice to *keeping borders in place and countries together*. This expressed, simultaneously, fears of "nationalist" disorders in a particularly explosive region, nervousness about spreading independence movements, and a preference for a strong, centralized state to manage the Yugoslav debt and the post-Communist transition. Germany by contrast viewed the fragmentation of Yugoslavia positively, at least as far as the two richest republics, Slovenia and Croatia, were concerned. However, both sides ended up adapting their positions pragmatically to a crisis whose dynamics escaped from their control.

Overall, up until June 1991 (on the eve of the declarations of independence), the main positions taken in public by U.S. or European governments supported Ante Markovic's neoliberal, federalist Yugoslav government against challenges from the republics.

Those expressing this antinationalism hardly troubled themselves about issues of identity or national rights, although these issues were raised by any effort to define a democratic Yugoslav project or to redefine countries. Western governments attributed little importance to tensions that were also at work from Rwanda to Quebec.

Beyond political and economic concerns, the key principle was the intangibility, or more exactly inviolability, of frontiers. But as soon as there was a disagreement about the frontiers, there was a "violation." Any unilateral declaration whatsoever was a violation of the principle. The new countries' governments—and the self-declared autonomous republics inside the new countries—have demanded each time that Western governments recognize the right to self-determination, i.e., to separation.

In practice, the fragmentation of Yugoslavia has meant permanent violation of the integrity of all the countries that have existed since the crisis began. Only *the country in question* has varied.

The integrity of ex-Yugoslavia was violated by Slovenia's and Croatia's unilateral declarations of independence, and later, at a time when the disintegration of ex-Yugoslavia had advanced further, by Bosnia-Herzegovina's and Macedonia's unilateral declarations of independence.

Croatia's integrity was violated (though Croatia was not yet recognized as independent at the time) by the unilateral declaration of the Serb Republic of Croatia (Krajina).

Just after Bosnia-Herzegovina organized its referendum on independence, its integrity was violated when Bosnian Serb nationalists decided to boycott Bosnian institutions and unilaterally declared the Serb Republic of Bosnia-Herzegovina. Its integrity was violated again by the unilateral declaration of the Croat Republic of Herceg-Bosna in July 1992, despite Tudjman's formal recognition of Bosnia-Herzegovina's integrity.

Serbia's integrity was violated after the Serbian authorities had abolished Kosovo's autonomy, when the province's Albanians decided to boycott the provincial elections and institutions controlled by Serbia and declared the Republic of Kosovo (while organizing parallel elections).

With the federation's crisis and fragmentation, civil wars (within the countries intially concerned) have continually turned into wars of aggression against newly created countries, carried out by governments now seen as foreign. Croatia's and Bosnia-Herzegovina's leaders hoped that winning international recognition would facilitate international intervention against outside Serbian aggression. Belgrade's response was to rely on the armed forces and internal uprisings in these two republics, and give equipment and logistical support to local Serb militias.

The substantial proportion of diaspora Serbs in the Yugoslav army, and the popular base that the Greater Serbian project has gained among Croatian and Bosnian Serbs, have provided evidence for the thesis (in part a reality) of an "ethnically based civil war." The role of the government and parties in Belgrade is thus formally reduced to that of outside support. Even as the Croatian government denounced Serbian policy in Croatia as an "outside aggression," it in fact acted in the same way toward Zagreb-backed Herceg-Bosna.

The creation of ethnically based countries came into conflict with the goal of keeping borders unchanged, and posed the issue of the right to self-determination to the "international community." The response was disjointed, hypocritical, and pragmatic. Each government adapted its "principles" to its own views of the "post-Communist order" and the Balkan troubles.

With the declarations of independence, in any event, it became impossible for Western governments to continue dealing with the issue like an ostrich sticking its head in the sand. A new "principle" was thus added to the first. But on what basis?

The "international community" tried at first to reconcile the two principles of the inviolability of frontiers and the right to self-determination. It "sufficed" to change the country in question, and acknowledge the right of self-determination only for the ex-federation's republics, i.e., only if the republics' borders were maintained—which meant no independence for Kosovo and no break-up of Croatia or Bosnia-Herzegovina.

Recognition of the new countries was however hemmed in by preconditions concerning minority rights. For a while, then, protection of minority rights was made a precondition—including for membership in the Council of Europe.

A commission of jurists was set up, named after its chairperson, Robert Badinter. The commission studied the situation in each republic that applied for recognition as an independent country. It issued a series of "opinions" that were sometimes favorable, sometimes unfavorable to recognition, depending on the rights granted to minorities and on international norms, accompanied by "recommendations." In fact the "opinions" given on this point by the Badinter Commission *were not respected* (except in Slovenia, which had no serious minority problem). There were no practical guarantees that Serb-Croat conflicts in Croatia would be settled, still less consensus among the three national communities in Bosnia-Herzegovina. These republics were nonetheless recognized, under German pressure, doubtless in a vain or naive hope of avoiding war.[6]

Be that as it may, the "international community" has done its best to recognize a right of separation only for ex-republics (whose borders it has tried to preserve, all its destructive "peace plans" notwithstanding), not for peoples, still less for minorities. On the juridical level, when the 1974 constitution gave a right of veto to the republics (but also to the provinces) it made them into sovereign entities whose borders could not be changed except by consensus; but that was also true for the federation's external borders. The legal hairsplitting covers up real conflicts. No peaceful solution can be imagined without a clear, explicit expression of these conflicts and the difficulties they involve. The conditions for applying self-determination in the Balkan context have not been forthrightly discussed. The Badinter Commission responded to a question from the Serbian government on Serb self-determination in Croatia and Bosnia[7] by saying simply,

> The Commission considers that international law, in its current state of development, does not lay out all the consequences of the right of self-determination. It is nonetheless well established that, whatever the circumstances, the right to self-determination cannot entail a modification of the frontiers existing at the time of independence.[8]

What is this in fact but a contradiction in terms?

International diplomacy has shifted its position drastically beginning with the Owen-Stoltenberg plan, which accepted Bosnia-Herzegovina's partition into three ethnic territories, whose inherent dynamic is to become three separate countries. This logic still dominated the "contact group's" negotiations in early 1995. However, the negotiators momentarily reject Croatian Serb separatism—and the separation increasingly demanded by the Albanians in Kosovo and Macedonia.

## These minorities who call themselves peoples

While the Serbs and Croats were constituent "nations" of ex-Yugoslavia, Kosovo's Albanians have the status of a minority. But they demand to be a people, with the rights of a people. Croatian independence and the changes to the Croatian constitution also turned the Croatian Serbs into a minority that refuses to be one. The "international community" will have trouble keeping to its "principle" of maintaining the ex-republics' old borders, since it has accepted the ethnic "peoples" in Bosnia-Herzegovina[9] as the basis for a redivision of the republic's territory. It will have a hard time eluding the problem of national minorities demanding recognition as "peoples" (nations) with countries of their own: the Kosovo Albanians and the Krajina Serbs of Croatia.

As the Kosovo Albanians make their case, they can emphasize that their province was a quasi-republic under the last Yugoslav constitution, granted equal rights of representation and veto in the federation. They can also emphasize their homogeneity, their cultural distinctiveness, and the size of their population, which is no less than that of other communities considered as "nations," such as Montenegro. They have organized a referendum which won massive backing from the population. But obviously if the Kosovo Albanians' right to separate is acknowledged, then the argument about borders falls apart, and with it the limitation of the right of self-determination to republics: and that would be giving in to the Serb position.

For the moment the Kosovo Albanians have peacefully demanded independence, but not the bringing together of Albanians in a single country. The affirmation of the "Greater Serbian" project will inevitably provoke heightened tensions in Kosovo and increase the real desire to reunite all Albanians.

Like all the communities the Albanians obviously vary, not only in their politics but according to whether they view the situation from Kosovo, Albania, or Macedonia. International pressures doubtless also have an impact on the positions they take. Albanian President Berisha said during his 1993 meeting with NATO representatives in Brussels that he is hostile to any "Greater Albanian" project.[10] His position and choice of words were challenged by the writer Rexhep Qosja, who considered that the phrase was pejorative and a product of Serb propaganda aimed at hiding the way that Albania's frontiers were imposed. According to Qosja the issue is not "conquering other people's land" but reconstituting an ethnic Albanian country with its borders and "its land." The writer said that the current borders are not "just" because they deny the Albanian people's right to unification. President Berisha answered by condemning any act of terrorist violence carried out in the name of Albanian reunification.[11] But the issue has been raised.

All Albanians demand at least recognition of a Kosovo republic and some form of autonomy for the Albanian communities in Montenegro and Macedonia. Macedonia's Albanians also demand recognition as one of the country's "constituent peoples." Greater Albania is not the only possible answer to the Albanian national question, any more than Greater Serbia is the only imaginable solution to the Serb national question.

The argument about "just" or "historic" borders has no "logical" limit in the Balkan region, which has been ravaged by one migration and empire after another. But it is true that the Albanian "ethnic frontiers" are "simpler" than the Serb ones, since Albanian-inhabited areas are contiguous and the populations more homogenous, while the Serbs have had to conquer "corridors" and "cleanse" ethnically mixed areas.

The tendency toward redrawing frontiers on an ethnic basis affects all the multinational countries and federations in the Balkans, Central and Eastern Europe, and the ex-USSR. It has to be systematically analyzed and dealt with, with all the socioeconomic, political (movements from above and from below), and cultural dimensions that it involves. Do some people have the right to self-determination but not others? Should this right be consigned to a bygone past? Or does it have to be rethought in a new context, in connection with the complex ways in which it is applied and with other fundamental rights? It is in any case hypocritical not to address the problem head-on and in a coherent way. Far from behaving forthrightly and coherently, the "international community" has presented its position in the form of "principles" that contradict each other and that have given rise to still other, shifting positions.[12] The treatment of Bosnia-Herzegovina is leading to fresh reinterpretations of the "principles" of the "international community."

## FROM REJECTING ETHNIC CLEANSING TO ORGANIZING IT

This flexibility of "principles" results from the negotiators' main concern. They are not interested in the real people and problems involved in the Yugoslav crisis. They have based their actions on the "governments that count" in order to "impose peace" (that is, their order) in the region.

For French and British diplomats after Slovenia's departure, the governments that counted were Serbia and Croatia. This is why the ambiguities of the Vance-Owen plan gave way to official acceptance in the Owen-Stoltenberg plan of Bosnia-Herzegovina's ethnically based division into "three countries." That remained the basic conception at work in the "peace plans" of early 1995.

Within this logic the Muslims or "Bosnians" are troublemakers—it is their fault that the war keeps going. The "safe havens" which UN forces promised to defend more "vigorously" bore a great resemblance to Indian reservations cut off from the world. The tragic episodes of Gorazde and the Bihac enclave demonstrated to the most reluctant onlookers what "vigorous defense" of these "safe havens" has amounted to, in light of Western governments' decision not to lose men in this war. But even if there had been a "vigorous defense" of these "safe havens," in what way would that be a "peace plan"? These enclaves symbolize the dead end of the plans for ethnic division of Bosnia.

Predictably this first European Muslim country, if it ever really sees the light of day, will be held in a stranglehold by the powers that are denouncing it in advance as "fundamentalist." It will most likely live under constant threat. Its neighbors will continually seek to enlarge their territories at its expense, in order to protect their borders or their "brothers under Muslim rule"—or simply in order to win a little more

*Lebensraum.* The Muslim state too would constantly need to find more *Lebensraum* for itself.

No one would want to be a minority in a situation in which there are no guarantees. Although building ethnically based countries can only multiply minority problems endlessly, the "international community" has played the sorcerer's apprentice in this regard. Opposing a partition that would create a Bosnian Muslim state, Tariq Haveric predicted its deadly consequences for the country labeled "Muslim":

> The population that will inhabit devastated Bosnia will consist above all of villagers.... By contrast, the majority of doctors, engineers, technicians, economists, and professors who have taken refuge in Western countries will not decide out of pure patriotism to return to this rump state, with all its economic and political uncertainties. Without them, Bosnia will fall back a hundred years.... There are too many Bosnians who have lost their whole families, who have been tortured or humiliated in Serb or Croat camps and who, now that the international community has betrayed them, will be a willing audience for extremism. Still worse, Izetbegovic, by signing the plan, will absolve the instigators of anti-Muslim genocide of any historic responsibility. They will always be able to say that the international community confirmed that they were right; that the coexistence of three peoples in a single country was never possible; and that the war was only a way to make the Muslims accept partition—which everyone had to admit in the end was the only logical solution.[13]

The Vance-Owen plan was unable to stop this partition, because it accepted, however obliquely, the idea that territorial separation on an ethnic basis was a safeguard and the only way to affirm the existence of distinct national communities. Some voices were raised in disagreement among the "great powers," of course. But what did the dissenters say and advocate?

There have been obvious, visible disagreements, of several different kinds. First, countries whose troops are actually involved on the ground (and easily taken hostage by Serb militias) are opposed by others (the United States and Germany) who say they want more "vigorous" blows against the "Serb aggressor." But on the purely military level (always supposing a clear goal for Western involvement in this war), it has often been stressed that without massive ground support to contain Serb counterattacks against UN enclaves and troops, stopping at air strikes would be impossible. The notion of "surgical strikes" that would not affect the civilian population (based on a fabricated image of the war in Iraq) is particularly irrelevant to a war where there is a definite popular base and where light, mobile weapons do most of the damage to the towns under siege.

The discordant notes between UN and NATO general staffs have also been stressed. But the contradictions are basically the same (and stay within the same limits) as the ones described above. The redefinition of NATO's functions in the "post-Communist period" is far from clear. Its intervention in Bosnia was envisaged as "the UN's armed force." Its credibility is at stake — and obviously undermined by a succession of ineffective "gestures." But the real problem is political. What exactly is NATO's "vigorous" intervention supposed to accomplish?

Those who call for NATO intervention present the war in Bosnia as a war by expansionist Serb fascism against an internationally recognized country. But the war is also linked to the *internal* division of Bosnia by the Bosnian parties in power. Besides, even if the crimes and horrors accompanying "ethnic cleansing" in Bosnia can be called fascistic, Serbs are not the only ones who commit them: the Croat nationalist destruction of Muslim Mostar is enough to make one shudder.

There was a real, acknowledged crisis of the old Yugoslav federation. There is also a real, acknowledged crisis of independent Bosnia. How can these crises be faced? How can the Bosnian communities be enabled to live together? Through a NATO military intervention against Serb targets?

The UN troops are involved on the ground with a mandate for "maintaining peace": a mandate for neutrality, in a situation of institutional crisis and open warfare. Still worse, the "peace" plans that these troops defend rely on the premise of territorial division; as long as no maps are set and no agreements are reached, this can only encourage fresh offensives. The powers denounce ethnic cleansing, of course, but their plans are "organizing" an ethnic division of mixed areas. The UN force's mandate is thus *unmanageable.* This results from a political choice: ethnic division as a solution, based on nationalist governments and warlords.

The United States has not challenged these basic choices in any coherent way. It has taken a certain distance, but only in keeping with its own strategic goals. These are the grounds on which it has raised criticisms of the (constantly changing) proposed plans: it is relying on different allies. The French and British, who advocate dividing Bosnia into three countries, basically count on an alliance between Milosevic and Tudjman. But *both sides' accounts of the nature of the war remain superficial and hypocritical.* The French and British governments are more explicit in accepting the aggressive dynamics of ethnic cleansing; but is Washington any more consistent, denouncing ethnic cleansing only when Serbs do it? We have in any event noted the inconsistency of U.S. positions on the Muslim-Croat federation.

A coherent alternative would have required: first, not leaving Bosnia's future in the hands of the nationalist parties alone, but giving the "civic" parties and councils a way to take part in the negotiations and to make their proposals known throughout Bosnia; second, carrying out a democratic process of self-determination, consulting first of all the populations concerned rather than the Zagreb and Belgrade governments; third, requiring as part of this democratic process pluralism in discussion, and arresting the paramilitary militias and notorious war criminals; fourth, systematically denouncing all ethnically discriminatory policies—not just the Serbs'; and fifth, treating the whole of the ex-Yugoslav crisis and the national questions involved in a systematic way—in particular, dealing with the Serb questions at the same time as the Albanian questions.

A critical evaluation of embargo policies should also be carried out. Both the embargo against Serbia and Montenegro and the arms embargo have been obviously counterproductive and hypocritical. Unfortunately they have left a difficult problem behind them.

The embargo against Serbia has not stopped the war, still less weakened Milosevic's government. The Serbian population has blamed the blockade, not the regime's policies, for the economic catastrophe. It has not made the task of the isolated democratic opposition any easier either. In addition, by one-sidedly taking Serbia to task, the embargo has consolidated Serb nationalism, one of whose unifying themes is portraying Serbs as victims of an international plot. Any policy that fails to denounce *all* those responsible for the conflict (apportioning the blame differently and unevenly among them) can only solder together what must be broken at all costs: the dynamic of nationalist unification that prevents any criticism, any pluralism, any negotiation, any compromise. The problem is that lifting the embargo now would almost certainly strengthen still more the Serbian government, which is most to blame for the war. These are the dead ends that ineffective policies lead to.

The hypocrisy of the other embargo—the arms embargo—no longer requires proof. In the war in Bosnia an embargo like this, which obviously hurt most the forces loyal to the Bosnian government, amounted to a cynical calculation: that the war could be ended by partitioning Bosnia between Serbs and Croats at the expense of the distinct Bosnian Muslim community. This was in addition an ignorant, stupid calculation. It assumed that there would be no resistance on the Bosnian side. Worse, it imagined that peace could be based on the liquidation of a whole community through ethnic cleansing or forced assimilation.

Demonizing Muslims as the new post-Communist enemy can doubtless facilitate this dirty job, particularly in the United States since the Gulf War as well as in France. But unjust policies also turn out to be ineffective, or at least provoke resistance, in the medium or long term. The threatened Bosnian Muslim community's *right to defend itself* must be recognized. All the more because no one else has defended it; and self-defense would allow it to struggle on both the fronts where it is threatened.

It is difficult to judge, through the eyes of the Bosnians themselves, what their possibilities for self-defense are at this late date. The "international community" is responsible for a terrifying mess in Bosnia. The UN force is at one and the same time a hostage of the extremist Serb militias and a partial protector of the populations under siege, who would see its withdrawal as a tragic abandonment. The divisions on the Serb side, whatever their limits, are another element in the relationship of forces. Everything possible should be done to exacerbate their divisions, for example by demanding that Milosevic disarm the paramilitary militias.

Meanwhile, some weapons have in fact been reaching the Bosnian forces—as they should: it is unfair to treat those defending people who are under siege in the same way as those doing the besieging. It is something thing else again to judge, from the standpoint of the people being fired on, what the situation is now and what the effect would be now of lifting the arms embargo on the Bosnians. President Izetbegovic has asked that the lifting of the arms embargo be postponed until at least May 1995, because he knows very well that the Bosnian army is incapable of defending the enclaves from which the

UN force would then withdraw. But the "liberation of Bosnia" is above all a political struggle against all the regressive policies that are assaulting, from without and within, the coexistence of communities.

Those policies spring from the idea of "ethnically pure" countries created through war. Is this a manifestation of Europe's past—or of its future?

## Conclusion

# Today Yugoslavia; Tomorrow Europe?

### WAITING FOR GODOT...

The dismemberment of Yugoslavia continues.

At the beginning of 1995, Bosnia-Herzegovina was in greater danger than ever of being partitioned into two different countries—or three, given the fragility of the Muslim-Croat federation. War could resume as well in Croatia, in areas (Krajina and Slavonia) controlled by Serb secessionists. The Kosovo issue remained explosive. Macedonia was still subject to the boycott by neighboring Greece, and internal tensions over the status of its Albanian minority.

Diplomatic initiatives were underway in an attempt to have new "peace plans" (i.e., shaky compromises) adopted before spring (the "good" season for military offensives). The logic of these "peace plans" was to try to prevent crystallization of a united Greater Serbia, to maintain at least formally the integrity of Croatia, Serbia, and Bosnia-Herzegovina, with mutual recognition of their borders. In exchange, the plans would undoubtedly offer: (a) a very large measure of autonomy for Serb-majority Krajina, and international trusteeship over other disputed areas that were controlled by Serb secessionists but had no prewar Serb majorities; (b) decentralization of Bosnia into two political entities (49 percent to be controlled by Radovan Karadzic's troops, 51 percent left over for the Muslim-Croat federation), which would have the right to form confederations with neighboring Croatia and Serbia; and (c) Kosovo's return to an autonomous status, or a proposed partition of the province between Serbs and Albanians.

The obstacles to acceptance of this kind of plan were well known. Serb extremist forces (still supported by the Orthodox Church) would reject any proposal that failed to recognize the self-proclaimed Serb republics as countries with the right to unite with one another; they would also not want to give up the project of claiming Kosovo as Serb land. The Kosovo Albanians on the other hand would not accept a façade of autonomy that would leave them subject in practice to the Belgrade government. Resistance would come as well from Croat extremist forces, who would not give up their project of expanding the Bosnian Croat state and winning back by force Croat areas controlled by Serb secessionists. Finally Alija Izetbegovic's SDA party, the Bosnian army, and the Bosnian presidency were and would increasingly be polarized between several currents: one favorably inclined toward a partition that would clearly establish a Muslim state, others seeking to keep the whole of Bosnian territory together at any price—hypothetically by means of a "war of liberation."

More substantially, the weakness of the "peace" proposals resulted from the fact that they embodied two contradictory dynamics. One dynamic tended to break the ex-Yugoslav region apart by "ethnically cleansing" it; the other dynamic tended by contrast to knit the region back together through a rapprochement among its communities. This second, unifying dynamic could only gather strength by proposing a regional plan for socioeconomic reconstruction and development; fighting against nationally and socially exclusionary policies within each country; prosecuting individuals in each community guilty of war crimes, without demonizing peoples but with complete openness about the dark pages of the past—in short, by working to reestablish confidence between communities. The least that can be said is that the negotiators showed no such intentions.

Whatever temporary political agreements may be reached, challenges to the oppressive and exclusionary policies of the governments in power must come essentially from their own *civil societies*. Forces exist and will continue to exist within civil society that are capable of resisting regressive policies and rulers. By contrast, those who base their hopes on foreign military intervention, or believe that progressive solutions to the Yugoslav crisis will come from the Western governments, are "waiting for Godot": waiting for something that will never come or will not be enough to solve the problems.

People *are* resisting the processes of national homogenization that are preventing pluralist democracy from functioning. There are independent media and civic movements that are fighting against chauvinism: antinationalist women's movements; independent trade unions; antiwar centers; organizations defending individual and collective rights. They may seem too laughably weak to support, given the scale of the war's horrors. Solidarity with them may do nothing to alleviate the sense of helplessness that drives many to seek escape in warmongering speeches. But support for independent forces is a precondition for the development of real alternative peace plans.

There is another Croatia, another Serbia, another Bosnia-Herzegovina that are resisting, though they are stifled. They must be enabled to express themselves. The international negotiators do not allow their voices to be heard, so the citizens' movements, in solidarity against policies of ethnic cleansing, must broadcast their own voices. They must keep alive a pluralist spectrum of projects that prepare the future. They must amplify the voices of the voiceless, those who want to live together and are not represented in the negotiations: the Serb Consultative Councils of Bosnia who deny Karadzic's right to speak in their name; Sarajevo's "Circle 99," whose petition against their city's partition had been signed at the beginning of 1995 by more than two thirds of Sarajevans.

But we must be clear. As long as the opposition to the reactionary policies now in force remains divided, without a coherent alternative program capable of mobilizing the region's peoples, no fundamental challenge will be possible to the current dynamic of negotiations with the powers that be.

Today's situation is dramatically different from the one the World War II-era Partisans faced. The Partisans began to organize antifascist resistance without any aid from the Allies—either from Stalin or from the West. The Western powers supported the resistance that fought for the Serb monarchy, whose troops on the ground (the Chetniks) practiced ethnic retaliation. More than a million people died in that war (in a country with fewer than 20 million inhabitants). Despite the deaths, despite the ethnic cleansing, despite their isolation, the Partisans managed to unify an armed resistance force of several hundred thousand people. What changed the course of events—and won the Allies' support—was not just the evidence of their victories and the growing force of their Committees of National Liberation. The conditions for their victory were political (the antifascist unity of the Yugoslav peoples in all their diversity; a federative project that was built in the course of the struggle) and social (cancellation of debts and distribution of land in the liberated areas gave the Partisan army its mass peasant base).

The main cause of the current dead ends is the lack of a credible socioeconomic and political alternative (on a Balkan as well as European scale) to the reactionary policies that now have the upper hand. This is not just a Yugoslav problem.

Is it too late? Undoubtedly. But not totally.

It is necessary to continue to reject the logic of ethnically "pure" countries, wherever they may arise: in Kosovo or Voivodina, in any of the Bosnian "republics" or enclaves, in Croatia, wherever. As Hungarian jurist Tibor Varady says, the issue of minorities is "both the cause of and the key to the conflicts." In the areas that are still ethnically mixed, "whatever we ask for our people among 'them,' we have to offer to 'their people' among us."[1] Peace cannot be built on a logic of exclusion.

The newly "independent" countries have a vital need to reestablish communication amongst themselves, at every level. Equitable and coherent solutions to the Balkan region's interlinked national and social issues can only be found by involving in the effort all the countries where the scattered peoples of the Balkans live. The risk remains real that this region riddled with historic fractures will go up in flames, though this is not in any great power's interest. The alternative would be a form of Balkan, or even Danubian, union of independent countries. It would at least allow borders to remain stable for a time *because* the borders would be open for the region's peoples: i.e., because rights to multiple citizenship and to free circulation of people would be assured.

We often hear that the Yugoslav region's communities have never coexisted except when an "outside" yoke (an empire, the Serbian monarchy, the Titoist regime) was imposed on them. But why not an *inner* cement: democracy for development? This would mean political, economic, and social democracy, fighting against the marginalization that unemployment and poverty create. Narrow or oppressive communalist withdrawals are responses to fears of social exclusion. The world economic crisis is spreading two-tier societies everywhere, or even writing off whole countries. Therefore it is not a matter of copying a model that worked somewhere else. We can only anticipate that the importance of frontiers will be inversely proportional to the extention of individual and collective democratic rights, and that the importance of frontiers will also diminish *as gaps in living standards decrease.* On all these levels, the issues in Yugoslavia are of universal importance.

## YUGOSLAV ISSUES, BALKAN ISSUES, OR UNIVERSAL ISSUES?

The confederalization of the Yugoslav system meant the establishment of consensus decisionmaking. But consensus is no longer possible once gaps in development are too great, and once economic incentives encourage "looking out for number one" and "might makes right." Market mechanisms deepen the gaps between developed and less developed regions. This disintegrative logic was at work in Czechoslovakia—and isn't it visible in the European Union as well as North America, in Belgium and Italy as well as Canada and Mexico, all of which have their rich Slovenias and their bargain basements? Yet they are all in danger of having their own Chiapas.

Redistributing resources in order to reduce inequality raises in turn the issue of who controls the budget. Hypercentralized, bureaucratic planning is a dead end: it leads to waste that hurts developed regions as well as the others, with each side concluding quickly (as we have seen many times) that the other is "exploiting" it. Beyond the statistics, the real problem fostering the selfishness of rich regions and the stagnation of the rest was in Yugoslavia, as elsewhere, bureaucratism, the lack of openness in the system, the lack of political democracy, and thus the inefficiency of redistributive mechanisms. Privatization resolves none of these problems; it exacerbates them by speeding up these societies' disintegration.

What the Yugoslav system lacked was *democracy as regulator,* controlling market and plan at the same time and determining the balance between market and plan, between public and private sectors, according to the needs to be satisfied. Socioeconomic inequalities between localities and regions, or between countries in a larger whole, cannot be bridged without an "economic policy." That requires institutions that have legitimacy and can be controlled as they manage resources in a redistributive way.

What is the "right level" at which to manage resources? Can supranational democracy exist without any means of controlling it? The answers cannot be general and ahistorical. Besides, the answers can be combined: space can evidently be divided in more than one way. If regions and localities can take their rightful place in a process of withering away of nation-states, a given region can also fit into several different frameworks: multilateral cooperative ties are being made around the Baltic, the Black Sea, and the Mediterranean, and in the Balkans. Balkan Europe can also be simultaneously oriented toward the other Europes: Central, Eastern, and Western.

Lack of democracy and inadequate economic tools have perverted self-management's progressive potential. Is this really just a problem of the Yugoslav past? Taylorism has demonstrated in other parts of the world the limits of the productivity it can deliver. Don't we hear now that the quality and efficiency of production can also be improved through training and participation, through workers' sense that they are social actors rather than outcasts on parole? Does the barbarism of the exclusionary relationships that prevail in the world market have to be accepted because they are "efficient"—according to this market's own criteria? But rejecting the barbarism of market criteria does not in itself supply the answers.

## WHAT KIND OF DEMOCRACY?

> The concept of democracy has to be rethought, not just in Yugoslavia but in Europe as well ... since democracy has never been envisioned to apply to everyone. Does it include everyone in the same way? If it does, then it necessarily puts people at a disadvantage who don't fit the norm, who have another starting point, women or minorities for example.[2]

Democracy should increase decisionmaking by the people concerned. But who are the "people concerned"? Individuals, classes, sexes, and national, regional, and international communities! Since each human being has many aspects, the full satisfaction of everyone's needs cannot be reached by a simple system of making and carrying out decisions. Citizens are both producers and consumers, involved in collective relationships at several different levels, and affected by different kinds of problems that develop within the context of space-time variables. In Yugoslavia, self-management suffered from atomization and too narrow a horizon.

In reflecting on what forms of democracy would be adequate to deal with this complexity, one of the major challenges is determining the "site" and the proper and effective mechanism of decisionmaking and control to resolve a given problem. Should democracy include a right to self-determination in whose name exclusionary wars are waged? Or, as certain schools of thought suggest, is democracy in contradiction with recognition of national rights?[3]

### The right to self-determination is ... a right

The Yugoslav case illustrates—contrary to those who endorse the newly independent countries—the fact that the nation-state is not necessarily, in all circumstances, the best way of defending the rights of peoples. In practice in the contemporary industrial world, in which urbanization and the lowering of political and economic barriers bring about ethnic blending, the policy of delineating ethnically homogeneous nation-states is regressive for both the majority peoples and the others.

This is why we have to avoid clouding the discussion through the common confusion of two distinct notions:
- the right of self-determination of ethnic peoples: i.e., their right to exist culturally and politically and to choose the forms in which they exist; and
- the particular solution of forming a nation-state based on the ethnic group in question: a solution that is sometimes imposed as the first or best when that is not always the case.

To fight against this solution when it is recognized as harmful does not mean denying the *right* to form an ethnic state. It must be demonstrated that this is not the best choice, in other words that other, better options exist. So there must be different ways of being a "people." Forming a separate country for one single ethnic group is not (and must not be) the only choice.

If we want to avoid political separation or the creation of new countries, we must develop a citizenship based on social, cultural, and political rights *that persuades people not to separate.* This is the only way for the community concerned to see the existence of a multinational country *as the safeguard of its freedom, its development, and its advancement*—and if the issue arises, it must have the right to a *collective representation independent of the different countries in which the community is dispersed.* This kind of collective representation is indispensable in any case for peoples who are always and everywhere in a minority, such as Roma (Gypsies).[4]

If defending the right to self-determination does not necessarily mean supporting the solution of building a nation-state, then a people must be able to defend its interests effectively in other ways. Building a country of multicultural and multiethnic (multinational) citizens is *one* form of self-determination. Such a country can be a federation or confederation if its peoples live in more or less distinct territories. But we have seen that in ex-Yugoslavia this territorialization (in cantons, provinces, or republics) is not always desirable.

The constitutional solutions advocated by civic forums in Bosnia-Herzegovina, based on two-chamber legislatures, are an example of how principles of egalitarian citizenship and equal, nonterritorially-based ethnic representation can be compatible with one another. The decentralization of a country into republics or historic regions[5] and home rule by local communities could eventually be combined with a system for representing nationalities at the local level if they ask for it.

A people's right to self-determination, understood as a *sovereign subject's right to choose among various alternative solutions*, expresses the right to resist oppression and to be treated with dignity as a community. Unity by force is counterproductive. But an ethnic country should be formed only if it is a community's only or best way to defend itself. Many criteria should be taken into account in making this judgment: not only relations with other communities, but also the socioeconomic and political context. A people's recognition and representation as a people will in any case ensure the free, voluntary character of the bonds that unite different peoples. This still of course leaves open the issue of the forms of representation and their control by the people concerned.

Far from being counterposed to the transcendence of nation-states, the recognition of peoples' right to sovereignty is a *precondition for peoples' mutual association*. A solid renunciation of a part of a people's sovereignty can only come as the result of a decision freely made on the basis of an understanding by all of the shared advantages of joint decisionmaking. This is why any project for living together in a common country is best defended by recognizing at one and the same time peoples' rights to integration, to difference, and to separation.

We have emphasized that both Serb and Croat nationalism refuse to other peoples the rights they demand for the communities they are supposedly defending. No nation (even if it is the most developed, the most populous, or the best armed) can be allowed to impose its own choice on others. A people's options for self-determination must be limited by the exercise of the same rights by other communities living on the same land.

But on the other hand, if the right to self-determination is limited to cases in which it can be exercised easily (when the nation in question is homogeneous and concentrated in a territory previously dominated by imperialism, for example) or in which it clearly has a progressive content, then it loses the character of a democratic right. Then pseudojuridical criteria are conjured up in order to avoid recognizing this right when it does not seem "appropriate." Or pseudoscientific definitions are invented of what a "nation" (a people with the right to self-determination) is, as opposed to a "national minority" or an ethnic group that "by definition" would not pose the issue of a separate country—that would not have the *right* to pose the issue.

## Peoples' rights, minority rights, individual rights

The right of nations—of peoples—to self-determination is generally counterposed to minority rights. Thus the right to self-determination is reduced to the right to form an independent country, or to merge with an existing nation-state after seceding as a minority from another country. Minority rights on the other hand imply acceptance of the framework constituted by a country identified with a distinct, majority national or ethnic group.

In fact the notion of "minorities" embraces all kinds of different situations. National communities that are in a minority inside a particular country's borders can make a great variety of different demands (cultural autonomy, political autonomy, individual rights, etc.). Various typologies have been proposed that will not be discussed here.[6] There is no airtight distinction in any case between the concepts (or situations) of minorities as opposed to those of "peoples." Borders will be challenged, violently, if oppression exists inside them: that, and not some *a priori* definition, is what brutally transforms a national minority or an ethnic group into a community that demands the rights of a nation.

As evidence for this conclusion, consider these cases: the three communities of Bosnia-Herzegovina (none of which has an absolute majority); the Kosovo Albanians, and the Croatian Serbs. Each case is in reality a *fragment of a people*. (The Muslim community is in danger of fragmentation even inside Bosnia-Herzegovina if it is "assigned" to enclaves cut off from one another.)

In the war being waged in ex-Yugoslavia, the governments, militias, and armies have imposed their own choices on the peoples and ethnic groups, in the name of collective self-determination. Of course it is not always possible for an oppressed people to organize democratic consultations, and self-determination is often carried out under constraint. But any kind of psychological or physical terrorism that victimizes individuals in the name of a group must be rejected, because it blocks free expression and free choice. Peoples' rights should not be defined in isolation from other rights, in particular from individual freedoms.

This is another reason why citizenship must be preserved and distinguished from nationality. Different identities must be given the space to express themselves. The right to an ethnically mixed identity or to integration in a multicultural society should be defended just as vigorously as the right to collective ethnic or national affirmation. People must stay free to call themselves "Serbs," "Croats," or "Muslims"—but also free to call themselves "Bosnians" or "Yugoslavs."

## *The Hungarian case*

Hungarians are one of the peoples in central and eastern Europe who are divided between several different countries (notably Romania and Slovakia, where there are real tensions). The break-up of the Austro-Hungarian empire, the formation of nation-states in its place, and the outcomes of wars left "nonethnic" borders behind them. The approach of the new Hungarian government in the mid-1990s (dominated by ex-Communists and liberals) is to defend Hungarian minorities in other countries, not by trying to push back Hungary's borders, but by granting rights to Hungary's minorities and urging others to reciprocate. This has stimulated Hungary to adopt a minority rights law that is probably one of the world's most advanced. Its approach is to further the distinction and articulation between citizenship and nationality. We reprint here a few extracts from Hungary's 1993 law "on the rights of national and ethnic minorities."

> One of the Law's premises is that the rights of national and ethnic minorities cannot be adequately affirmed in the framework of individual civil rights alone. It follows that it is important that these rights also be defined as collective rights.

The Law guarantees minorities, as an important collective right, the possibility of establishing their autonomous minority associations ... at both local and national levels. The Law includes material guarantees for the realization of the rights that it defines; it lays down rules for this purpose for funding from multiple sources....

The legal system, besides tolerating, also facilitates the protection of minority identities. [It guarantees] the freedom to choose one's own identity as well as equal rights for minorities.[7]

### Collective rights

The idea of a "collective identity" should be treated cautiously in any case, and distinguished from the idea of *collective rights.* Identity is really a very subjective thing. A single individual's identity is complicated enough; the idea of "identity" becomes all the more problematic when applied to groups. We have to be careful to avoid letting a few people "define" the identity of a whole group, which can lead very quickly toward imposing norms on a whole group. These norms usually amount to an evaluation in which evolving historical and cultural traits are declared "natural."

When nationalism (or for that matter feminism) abandons the *defense of collective rights* in order to impose a checklist for "collective identity" ("national identity" or "women's identity"), people are in danger of being labeled and rejected based on whether or not they are "authentic" ("true Serbs," "true Croats," "real women"). People affirm their identity all the more strongly and provocatively because they are struggling for something that has been forbidden or repressed. So oppressed communities' struggles for national existence, identity, self-organization, or the right to be different must not be confounded with exclusionary models imposed by dominant communities. But defending the right to claim an identity that has been stifled or denigrated does not require accepting new straitjackets.

Individuals' rights to free choice of their own identities are essential in the face of such homogenizing tendencies. This is not a plea for individualism. On the contrary, individual freedom is a precondition for any freely chosen commitment to a collective movement. In this way the movement can be saved from closing in on itself in a way that would prevent its taking account of its members' changing situations and needs. The group's richness is in its pluralism, which allows the group to resist apartheid-like situations.

When it comes to national questions, functioning by consensus (with each community guaranteed a right of veto on issues that are of essential concern to it) is more progressive than majority-rule democracy. This is why *the concept of "minorities" should be replaced by the concept of "national communities" or "ethnic communities"* (whose worth and the defense of whose rights *do not depend on numbers*). This approach makes sense only if the differences among communities are seen in their richness as something to be energized, not just preserved—to be sure, without the creation of ghettos or "particularisms" opposed to the identity of the "others," or to learning the "others'" languages.[8]

Democracy conceived as a system of, by, and for citizens, based on the rights of individuals, is often posed as the alternative to the rise of exclusionary nationalisms. Missing here is an understanding of how nationalism can be a reaction against an overly abstract conception of democracy that overlooks collective rights, demands, and requirements. Yet while the rights of peoples are an important element of democracy, exclusionary nationalism—even the exclusionary nationalism of oppressed nations—is the negation of pluralism, from the moment that it seeks to create homogeneity. The challenge is to fight against exclusionary nationalism without rejecting peoples' rights. The distinction is important in confronting the explosion of reactionary nationalisms.

There is a dark (exclusionary and racist) side and a bright (democratic and pluralist) side to national movements, as Michel Wieviorka rightly explains.[9] The political and cultural awakening of Mexico's Indians offer a look at the bright side. Their recent declaration is a magnificent illustration of a possible democracy still to be invented.

> For more than 500 years, Mexico's Indian peoples have suffered from marginalization, poverty, discrimination, exclusion, contempt for the cultural forms of our social relations and community life....
>
> Experience has clearly shown over the past five centuries that programs give no fundamental and lasting solutions to our situation of marginality and poverty if they are not based on indigenous peoples' participation on the basis of their own conceptions, and carried out under their own authority with adequate power.... The current system of political organization, the current regime (centralized, exclusionary, authoritarian, homogenizing, and rejecting of pluralism), must be replaced with a state of autonomous entities,

which will make possible respect for diversity and open the door for Indian people's participation in defining a country for everybody.

The autonomy that we call for is not a project for exclusion, nor something divorced from the deep aspiration of the majority of Mexicans who want democracy, justice, and freedom.... Our overarching political project for autonomy is also in no way meant to exclude regions or areas where several groups live together. It proposes for these regions ... the possibility of living together in unity and diversity, equality and mutual respect. This means the establishment of multicultural or multiethnic regions....

We want to find a solution for everyone in the framework of the integrity of the larger Mexican nation.... The autonomy that we propose involves establishing forms of communal, municipal, and regional self-government, autonomous regions, in the framework of national unity. Our autonomy project is thus not a separatist proposal, which we Indian peoples would consider a sterile idea....

Autonomy is the basis of our way of life. Our basic project aims at transforming these practices and ways of life into part of the country's political system.... But ... we do not want the government to continue turning our communities into reservations where peoples are discriminated against, or to continue cutting us off from the rest of the country.... The community is the foundation of autonomy, but autonomy goes beyond the community, by working to join peoples together through self-government at a regional level....

We want to create autonomous regions where human rights and peoples' cultural, political, and social rights are respected ... and where peoples represented by their autonomous governments devote themselves to solving their communities' and regions' social and economic problems. We want to take part with our own representatives in the political institutions and federative entities in which our autonomous regions must take their place.... In short, we want genuinely to participate, through our own autonomous structures, in the Mexican nation and fatherland.[10]

## THE CLASH OF TWO CRISES

Is the nationalist fragmentation now underway exclusively or even primarily inherited from the "Communist" regimes?[11]

In reality it is the result of *two* crises, not just of the "socialist bloc's" collapse. The rise of racism and of far right parties like Jean-Marie Le Pen's National Front in France is not an "infection" by a virus from the East. Deepening inequality and exclusionary policies are the result of neoliberal responses to the end of thirty years of growth and the crisis of the welfare state, a crisis that began in the early 1970s *in the West.*

It is the worldwide return to nineteenth century capitalism that fuels privatization in the East. Privatization means taking over territory and resources: i.e., wars, in ex-Yugoslavia as in the Caucasus. There neoliberal policies have led, in poorer regions facing a destructive world market, to protectionist nationalism. In rich regions like the Czech Republic by contrast, neoliberalism has led to a nationalism aimed at "dumping"[12] poor regions in order to secure a better market position. The socioeconomic hardships caused by these policies tend to provoke defensive reflexes: attempts to keep the policies' victims, primarily "foreigners," on the other side of the border.

Free market competition for profit in a world of haves and have-nots imposes its own "totalitarianism." Relationships of social and national oppression, as cruel and inefficient as bureaucratic centralism, are hidden behind the apparently objective working of supply and demand.

The collapse of the "socialist camp," far from giving capitalism a way out of its crisis, has introduced new sources of instability, regional crises, and even wars, and a tide of refugees. The clash of the two systems' crises is embodied in the cost of German unification and its destabilizing effects on the European Union. At the same time the opening to the West has not met Eastern Europeans' expectations that free market policies would mean efficiency and democracy.[13]

In the East as in the West, the traditional dividing lines have been scrambled for lack of clear perspective. In a time of crisis the nation-state protects the good (advanced welfare states) along with the bad (narrow, exclusionary nationalism), for several reasons. Free market Europe deepens inequalities; makes countries compete with one another to make deeper social cutbacks; sends social and national policies spiralling backwards; and enthrones a supranational, "soulless," and "faceless" technocracy. To borrow the words of writer Predrag Matvejevic:

> It is to be hoped that the Europe of the future will be less Eurocentric than the Europe of the past was, more open to the third world than colonialist Europe was, less egoistic than the Europe of separate nations was, and more conscious of its "European spirit," less prone

to Americanization. It would be utopian to expect Europe in the foreseeable future to become more cultural than commercial, less fragmented and more cosmopolitan, more understanding than arrogant, less haughty and more welcoming, and finally—why not?—to have a bit more socialism with a human face and a bit less faceless capitalism.[14]

The international and European communities' failure in ex-Yugoslavia will have consequences elsewhere. But it is itself the consequence of what these communities are: of their own inability to exist in a form that is inclusive and egalitarian, that fosters solidarity and genuinely embodies progressive values.

Inventing a genuine economic, social, cultural, and political democracy, capable of subordinating social organization to human needs, is no easy task in an increasingly globalized economy, in which the most "efficient" thing to do is the most socially regressive. We cannot resist this economy by dividing our forces: erecting new barricades to protect the haves from the have-nots, the "civilized" nations from the "Balkans," Fortress Europe or Fortress America from the immigrants.

Even if there are no more easy answers, we must at least keep a radical, critical spirit alive in face of a world disorder that will increasingly have to camouflage its failures with more and more "humanitarian" military interventions.

# Chronological Appendix

### A. The Middle Ages

**500-600**   Slavs arrive in Balkans, where Albanians of Illyrian origin already lived.

**800-1100**   First Bulgarian empire. Christian missions reach Balkans from Rome and Constantinople. Schism between Rome and Constantinople: Slovenes, Croats, and Bosnians become Roman Catholic; Serbs, Montenegrins, and Macedonians come under Eastern Orthodox Church.

**900-1100**   Kingdom of Croatia.

**1100-1200**   "Personal union" of Hungarian and Croatian monarchies. In conflicts with Hungary, Bosnia is accused of "heresy." A "Bosnian" church grows up distinct from Catholicism and Orthodoxy. Second Bulgarian empire.

**1100-1400**   Kingdom of Serbia. Kingdom of Bosnia. Slovenes, already included in the Holy Roman (German) Empire, come under Austrian Habsburg rule.

### B. The Ottoman and Austro-Hungarian Empires

**1300-1400**   Ottomans conquer Macedonia and Albania.

**1389**   Turkish victory over Serbs at the battle of Kosovo. Ottomans conquer Serbia.

**1463**   Turkish conquest of Bosnia. Many Bosnians become Muslim.

**1526**   Parts of Hungary, including Slavonia, come under Ottoman rule. Other parts of Hungary and Croatia come under Austrian Habsburg rule.

**1554**   Bosnia, previously divided into districts, becomes an Ottoman province.

**1500-1700**   Turkish siege of Vienna (Austria). Austro-Turkish war. Serb migrations.

**1500-1600** Creation of "Croatian military frontier" (Serb Krajina).
**1804-1817** Serb revolts against the Ottoman empire.
**1809-1815** Napoleon abolishes republic of Dubrovnik and annexes "Illyrian provinces" to the French empire.
**1830** Serbia becomes autonomous within the Ottoman empire.
**1878** League of Prizren: Albanians demand autonomy within Ottoman empire. Treaty of San Stephano. Congress of Berlin. Recognition of Serbian independence. Austria occupies Bosnia-Herzegovina.
**1908** Austria annexes Bosnia-Herzegovina. Orthodox and Muslims get political and cultural autonomy.
**1912** First Balkan War (against Turkey). Recognition of independent Albania.
**1913** Second Balkan War (against Bulgaria). Serbia acquires Kosovo and Macedonia.
**1914** Assassination in Sarajevo. World War I begins.

### C. From the First to the Second World War

**1918 November:** Allied victory ends World War I.
**December 1:** Creation of the Kingdom of Serbs, Croats, and Slovenes.
**1920** Constituent Assembly elections. Communist Party comes in third (winning fifty-nine deputies). Communist Party and unions it leads are banned.
**1921** Adoption of a centralist constitution, rejected by the Croats. Administrative redivision of the country.
**1928** Assassination of three Croat deputies, including Croat Peasant Party leader Stjepan Radic.
**1929 January 6:** Coup d'état by King Alexander. The country is renamed Yugoslavia.
**1934** Assassination of King Alexander in Marseilles. Prince Paul becomes regent. A cabinet led by Stojadinovic, favorable to the Rome-Berlin axis, takes office.
**1939** Prime Minister Stojadinovic is replaced by Cvetkovic. A Serb-Croat compromise creates an autonomous "Croat Banovina," including part of Bosnia-Herzegovina (which does not formally exist in this first Yugoslavia, which has no republics).
**1941** Yugoslavia joins Tripartite Pact between Germany, Italy, and Japan.
**March 27:** Anti-Tripartite Pact coup d'état overthrows Prince John in Belgrade.

**April 6:** Germany and Italy invade Yugoslavia and bomb Belgrade. Yugoslavia partitioned between Germany, Italy, and Bulgaria. Greater Albania (including Kosovo) is formed under Italian and German control.

**April 10:** Proclamation of the "Independent Croat State," which includes Bosnia-Herzegovina but not Dalmatia (annexed by Italy). Serbia is ruled by Serb quisling General Nedic. Draza Mihailovic's Chetniks (royalist and anticommunist) and Communist-led Partisans launch resistance. Partisans are forced to flee Serbia. Allies recognize only Chetnik resistance.

**1942** Creation in Bihac (in northern Bosnia) of the Antifascist Committee, embryo of a Communist-dominated provisional government. Communist Party and Committees of National Liberation acquire federative structure that prefigures future republics.

**1943** Creation in Jajce (in northern Bosnia) of the Antifascist Committee of National Liberation (AVNOJ), founding moment of a federative Yugoslavia. It refuses to let king return. British send mission to Yugoslavia: Partisans are recognized as only anti-fascist resistance.

**1944** Churchill meets Stalin: they agree Yugoslavia will be a monarchy (with fifty-fifty Soviet/Western influence).

**September 20:** Tito's army liberates Belgrade (ahead of the Soviet army). King (a refugee in London) has to recognize Tito as head of Yugoslav armies.

**1945 March 25:** Under Allied pressure, compromise is signed making Tito head of royalist government.

**Spring:** Churchill-Stalin deal is confirmed at Yalta.

**May 25:** War ends in Yugoslavia. Royalist ministers in London resign.

**November:** Opposition boycotts elections. Monarchy is abolished.

## D. Tito's Yugoslavia

**1948 June 28:** The Kremlin's first public resolution on the situation in Yugoslavia urges "the healthy forces in the Yugoslav Communist Party to impose a new political line on the leadership."

**1949 May:** Lazlo Rajk is arrested in Hungary. His "confession" supposedly proves that "the Tito clique has never had anything in common with either socialism or democracy."

**November:** Cominform meeting. From now on the CPY is characterized as a "clique" that has gone "from bourgeois nationalism to fascism" and "direct treason against the national interests of Yugoslavia." Milovan Djilas analyzes the Soviet Communist Party's bureaucratic degeneration.

**1949-1953** Since Moscow sees maintenance of private agriculture as "proof" of the CPY's "procapitalist" orientation, the Yugoslav regime tries to "answer" this accusation by adopting a policy of forcible collectivization.

**1950 June 27:** Adoption of law on workers' self-management.

**1952 November:** CPY's Sixth Congress decides to transform it into the League of Communists of Yugoslavia (LCY), and broadens self-management.

**1953** Stalin dies in the USSR. In Yugoslavia, reestablishment of private property on 80 percent of the land (limited to ten hectares, with a limit of five waged workers).

**1954 January:** Trial of Milovan Djilas.

**1955 May 26:** Khrushchev visits Yugoslavia to bring about reconciliation between the two countries. He makes a public self-criticism that Tito considers inadequate. Tito will never accept the idea of a socialist "camp" consisting only of Communist parties and subordinated to the Soviet party.

**1956** Second meeting of the Nonaligned Movement, founded the previous year in Bandung (Indonesia), at Brioni (Yugoslavia).

**1958 April:** LCY's Seventh Congress: after the Hungarian and Polish events, the congress declares that workers' self-management is a goal of the revolution everywhere and not only the "Yugoslav road."

**1960** World congress of 81 Communist parties denounces Yugoslav "opportunism" once more.

**1965** Introduction of an economic reform moving toward decentralization gives much greater leeway to market forces.

**1966** Dismissal of Communist leader Rankovic, one of the strongest advocates of a centralist Yugoslav regime (particularly in Kosovo).

**1968** Student revolt, workers' strikes, and a trade union congress that harshly criticizes the regime's economic policies. Denunciation of "development of capitalist relations of production" and of "wild" privatization. Condemnation of Soviet intervention in Czechoslovakia. Disturbances in Kosovo.

**1971 May:** Second LCY Congress focused on self-management (but very top-down). Denunciation of "centrifugal forces."

# CHRONOLOGICAL APPENDIX

**1971-1972 Winter:** Development of Croat nationalist movement ("Croatian Spring"). Repression and purges in Croatia, then purges in the other republics.

**1972 October:** Mini-"cultural revolution." Letter from Tito launches a campaign "against the millionaires" and for reorganization of the party.

**1973-1974** Kardelj criticizes "falling away from the dictatorship of the proletariat." Attacks on Milovan Djilas, supposedly to blame for the "errors" of the Sixth Congress, and on professors around *Praxis* in Belgrade, who are defended by their students. Campaign against "Cominformists" (accused of having factional ties to the Kremlin).

**1974 February:** A new constitution is adopted, providing for a collective presidency, equal representation of republics and autonomous provinces, and a right of veto. The army's role in the party and state is strengthened. A new system of delegations replaces the old system of deputies to different houses of the Federal Assembly. Bosnia is defined as a state of three equal peoples: Muslim, Serb, and Croat.

**May-June:** The LCY's Tenth Congress criticizes "illusions concerning the market" and affirms the need for strict party discipline and strengthening of the party's centralizing role at all economic levels.

**1976** Adoption of the "Law of Associated Labor," which breaks down enterprises into small units managing their own budgets and deciding how to divide their income among immediate individual income, collective consumption and investments. A new system of contractual planning is installed.

**1980** Tito dies. $20 billion foreign debt is publicly revealed.

### E. From Crisis to Collapse

**1981** Disturbances in Kosovo, with socioeconomic and political demands (e.g., a separate republic).

**1983** Milka Planinc government tries to implement austerity plan based on International Monetary Fund precepts. Inflation (already double-digit) increases, as does unemployment (2 percent in Slovenia, over 20 percent in Kosovo). Strike waves spread. The foreign debt persists. Living standards continue to fall.

**1986** Slobodan Milosevic becomes first secretary of the Communist League of Serbia. Ivan Stambolic, a moderate, becomes president of Serbia. The Serbian Academy of Sciences drafts a (nonpublic) Memorandum, portraying Serbs as victims of the Titoist regime and 1974 constitution. A press campaign swells against "threats of anti-Serb genocide" in Kosovo.

**1987** Political and financial scandal at Agrokomerk, whose chief executive officer is Fikret Abdic, a Bosnian. Serbian President Ivan Stambolic resigns. Milosevic takes control of Serbia.

**1988** Demonstrations against the military trial of antimilitarist movement leader Janesz Jansa (later defense minister of independent Slovenia). Pro-Milosevic, "antibureaucratic" mass demonstrations in Montenegro and Voivodina. Leaderships resign, and Milosevic extends power in Montenegro and Voivodina. A million people demonstrate in Belgrade against the "anti-Serb genocide" supposedly being perpetrated in Kosovo. Miners' strikes, disturbances, and purges in Kosovo. Removal of Albanian leader Azem Vllasi.

**December:** Mikulic's government resigns.

**1989 January:** Ante Markovic forms a new federal government. "Shock therapy" launched to curb hyperinflation, which has reached triple digits. Vukovar workers demonstrate in Belgrade and call for a Yugoslav-wide general strike.

**March 28:** Constitutional reform in Serbia challenges provinces' (Kosovo's and Voivodina's) autonomy.

**May:** Formation of anticommunist HDZ ("Croat Democratic Community") coalition led by Franjo Tudjman.

**June 28:** Mass demonstrations in Serbia on 600th anniversary of battle of Kosovo.

**September:** Pluralism develops in Slovenia: party's leading role is abolished and right to secede reaffirmed.

**1990 January:** Austerity policy against inflation. Last congress of League of Yugoslav Communists abandons party's leading role, but Slovenes break away and congress is adjourned.

**March 1:** State of emergency in Kosovo.

**April-May:** Free elections in Croatia (HDZ 42 percent, ex-Communists 25 percent). Formation of homogeneous HDZ government. HDZ leader Franjo Tudjman is elected president. Free elections in Slovenia, won by DEMOS coalition (55 percent as against 17 percent for Communists). Communist candidate Milan Kucan defeats DEMOS candidate Zoze Pucnik to win presidency. Preparations for a new Slovenian currency.

**June:** Serbian Assembly suspends Kosovo's government and parliament.

**July:** Secret meeting of Kosovo Albanian deputies declares Kosovo Republic separated from Serbia. Constitutional amendments in Croatia adopt chessboard flag and "Croat" as official language. Local referendum on Croatian Serb autonomy.

**November-December:** New Croatian constitution changes Croatian Serbs' status. Elections in Macedonia, with no party winning an absolute majority; Communist Kiro Gligorov elected president. Elections in Bosnia: 55 percent for the three nationalist parties (Muslim SDA, Serb SDS, and Croat HDZ), 25 percent for non-nationalist parties (ex-Communists, Liberals, and Reformists), 20 percent abstaining. Pact between the three nationalist parties: they elect a Muslim president (Alija Izetbegovic), a Serb speaker of parliament (Mocilo Krajisnik), and a Croat prime minister (Jure Pelivan). Elections in Serbia and Montenegro. Slobodan Milosevic is elected president with 65 percent of the vote, and his Socialist Party wins 194 out of 250 Assembly seats. Communist Momir Bulatovic is elected president of Montenegro. Referendum on independence in Slovenia.

**1991 January:** The Yugoslav Bank is found is to be printing money secretly, contrary to the Markovic Plan.

**March 9:** Anti-Milosevic opposition and many young people demonstrate in Belgrade, particularly for freedom of the press; the army intervenes.

**March:** Tudjman and Milosevic meet "secretly" at Karadjordje and discuss territorial partition, particularly of Bosnia-Herzegovina. Armed conflicts break out in Croatia: first deaths occur.

**May 2:** Croat police massacred in Croatia, probably by Serb militias.

**May 12:** Referendum in Serb Krajina declares that it will separate from Croatia and remain part of Yugoslavia.

**May 15:** Term of Federal President Jovic (a Serb) ends; the Serbs refuse to elect the Croat Stipe Mesic, whose turn it is according to the constitutional rotation, since Mesic has not concealed his hostility to maintaining the Yugoslav federation.

**May 19:** Referendum on sovereignty in Croatia.

**June 25-26:** Slovenia and Croatia declare independence.

**June 27:** Yugoslav army intervenes in Slovenia.

**July 5:** European Community begins arms embargo and freezes economic aid to Yugoslavia.

**July 7:** Brioni agreements reached through European mediation

provide for three-month moratorium on independence and election of Stipe Mesic to the Yugoslav presidency.
**July 18:** Collective presidency announces army's withdrawal from Slovenia over following three months. Purges and desertions.
**August 26-November 17:** Serb militias backed by army attack, lay siege to, and destroy ("liberate") multiethnic Vukovar in Slavonia.
**September 8:** Referendum on sovereignty in Macedonia.
**September 25:** UN Security Council adopts embargo on arms sales to Yugoslavia.
**October 3:** War spreads to one third of Croatia. Attack on Dubrovnik. "Serb bloc" (Serbia, Montenegro, Voivodina, and Kosovo, whose delegates are all controlled by the Serbian government) takes over Yugoslav collective presidency, declaring "imminent danger of war."
**October 7:** Moratorium ends; Slovenian and Croatian independence are confirmed.
**October 15:** Bosnian parliament votes for sovereignty.
**December 19:** European Community foreign ministers to decide to recognize newly independent countries if they meet criteria set by the Badinter Commission.
**December 23:** Germany recognizes Slovenian and Croatian independence.

## F. War

**1992 January 15:** Rest of European Community recognizes Slovenian and Croatian independence.
**January:** Act confirming Yugoslav federation's dissolution is officially signed in Zagreb. During HDZ (Tudjman) party congress, right wing in favor of ethnic partition of Bosnia-Herzegovina removes Stjepan Kljujic, a Bosnian Croat who opposes this policy, from HDZ leadership. He is replaced by Mate Boban, backed by Franjo Tudjman, and Croatian Defense Minister Gojko Susak (a Herzegovina native who had returned from exile in Canada).
**February 21:** UN Security Council decides to send 14,000 troops (UNPROFOR) to three Serb-controlled areas of Croatia, which are put under temporary UN protection.
**February 29-March 1:** Kosovo Albanians vote for independence in clandestine referendum. Referendum in Bosnia-Herzegovina on independence. Boycott by Serbs (33 percent of the population). The

# CHRONOLOGICAL APPENDIX

remaining 63 percent vote in favor. First clashes. Referendum in Montenegro for staying part of Yugoslavia.

**March 9:** Cutilhero plan for "ethnic cantonization" of Bosnia-Herzegovina, more or less supported by Serbs and Croats. Bosnian Muslims express hostility after President Izetbegovic accepts.

**April 6:** The European Community recognizes Bosnia-Herzegovina (despite Badinter Commission advice); Greece vetoes recognition of Macedonia (despite positive recommendation by Badinter Commission).

**April 7:** United States recognizes Croatia, Slovenia, and Bosnia-Herzegovina.

**Late April:** Siege of Sarajevo begins.

**April 27:** Serbia and Montenegro declare Federal Republic of Yugoslavia (the "third Yugoslavia").

**May 6:** "Secret" meeting between Mate Boban (Croat head of Tudjman's HDZ party) and Radovan Karadzic in Graz in Austria. They reach agreement on partitioning Bosnia-Herzegovina.

**May 22:** Bosnia-Herzegovina, Croatia, and Slovenia join the UN.

**May 30:** Commercial, oil, and air embargo against Serbia and Montenegro begins.

**May 31:** Slobodan Milosevic's Socialist Party wins legislative elections in new Yugoslavia. Milosevic's extreme right ally Vojislav Seselj's Serb Radical Party wins 30 percent. Opposition boycotts elections.

**June 15:** Serb writer Dobrica Cosic is elected president of the new Yugoslavia (Serbian-Montenegrin federation).

**June 16:** Croatia recognizes Bosnian independence.

**June 17:** Croatia and Bosnia-Herzegovina sign military alliance and call for military intervention against Serbia.

**July 2:** Milan Panic becomes prime minister of the Federal Republic of Yugoslavia.

**July 3:** Proclamation of "Herceg-Bosna," Croat republic within Bosnia-Herzegovina, led by Mate Boban.

**July 21:** Friendship pact between Croatia and Bosnia-Herzegovina.

**August 3:** Tudjman, reelected with 57 percent of the vote, wins first elections in independent Croatia.

**August 27:** International conference on ex-Yugoslavia in London establishes "permanent conference."

**September 3:** "Permanent conference" holds first session in Geneva, presided over by Lord Owen (EEC) and Cyrus Vance (UN).

**September 24:** UN General Assembly refuses to grant ex-Yugoslavia's seat to the new Serbian-Montenegrin federation.
**October 9:** UN Security Council declares no-flight zone over Bosnia-Herzegovina.
**October 17:** First Croat-Muslim clashes in Bosnia.
**December 8:** Legislative elections in Slovenia. Milan Kucan is re-elected president with 60 percent of the vote.
**December 18-20:** Legislative and presidential elections in Serbia. Milosevic in alliance with extreme right defeats Milan Panic for Serbian presidency, and soon afterwards ousts Panic as Yugoslav prime minister.
**1993 January 2:** Vance-Owen Plan is presented in Geneva: it proposes dividing Bosnia into ten provinces (three Serb, three Croat, three Muslim, with special status for Sarajevo). Croats accept proposal, Serbs and Muslims reject it. Negotiations are adjourned.
**February 10:** United States comes out in support of Vance-Owen Plan.
**February 19:** UN Security Council adopts Resolution 807, authorizing UN troops to use force to ensure their safety.
**February 22:** UN Security Council unanimously adopts Resolution 808, proposed by France, which creates an international criminal tribunal to judge those accused of war crimes in ex-Yugoslavia.
**February 25:** President Bill Clinton gives green light for dropping supplies by parachute in eastern Bosnia under U.S. command.
**March 11:** UN Protection Force (UNPROFOR) Commander-in-Chief General Philippe Morillon accepts remaining blockaded in Srebrenica, a Muslim enclave under siege by Serb forces.
**March 25:** Bosnian President Alija Izetbegovic signs Vance-Owen Plan, which Serbs still reject.
**March 31:** UN Security Council adopts Resolution 816, authorizing use of force to enforce no-flight zone over Bosnia-Herzegovina.
**April 6:** Croat offensive in Mostar aimed at "cleansing" it of Muslims in order to make it the "Croat capital" of Herceg-Bosna. Fighting breaks out between Croats and Muslims on new fronts in central Bosnia.
**April 8:** German Constitutional Court in Karlsruhe allows Germans to take part in NATO flights over Bosnian territory. Macedonia admitted to UN as "former Yugoslav republic of Macedonia."
**May 1:** Thorvald Stoltenberg replaces Cyrus Vance in negotiations.

**May 1-2:** At Athens summit, Bosnian Serb leader Karadzic under pressure from Slobodan Milosevic and Greek envoys agrees to sign Vance-Owen Plan, provided it is ratified by Bosnian Serb "parliament"—which rejects it and leaves the final decision to a referendum called for May 15-16.

**May 6:** Yugoslav (Serbian-Montenegrin) federation declares economic embargo against Bosnian Serbs to make them accept Vance-Owen Plan. UN Security Council adopts Resolution 824, making five new Bosnian cities (Sarajevo, Tuzla, Zepa, Gorazde, and Bihac) "safe havens."

**May 15-16:** Bosnian Serbs vote by 96 percent in referendum against Vance-Owen Plan and for independence of "Serb Republic of Bosnia-Herzegovina."

**May 31:** Yugoslav President Dobrica Cosic is ousted by Slobodan Milosevic's followers allied with Vojislav Seselj's ultranationalist Radical Party.

**June:** Bosnian Army Chief of Staff Sefer Halilovic is criticized for "adventurist actions." Other military chiefs are arrested in Sarajevo for "criminal" activity.

**June 15-16:** Serbian President Milosevic and Croatian President Tudjman demand in Geneva that Bosnia-Herzegovina be partitioned into three confederated ethnic entities. This new plan, backed by Owen and Stoltenberg, is rejected by Alija Izetbegovic.

**June 19-20:** Serbs in self-declared Serb Republic of Krajina in Croatia vote in referendum for unification with Bosnian Serbs.

**June 24:** Bosnian Serb and Croat leaders Karadzic and Boban endorse Milosevic's and Tudjman's proposal, burying Vance-Owen Plan.

**June 25:** Serb technocrat Zoran Lilic becomes president of Yugoslavia.

**August 20:** International mediators submit Owen-Stoltenberg Plan, which proposes dividing Bosnia into three republics: Serb (52 percent), Muslim (30) and Croat (18). Sarajevo would be under UN mandate, Mostar under EEC control. Alija Izetbegovic expresses reservations and demands access to the sea and guarantees for the "Muslim" state's viability and protection. Croat Herceg-Bosna functions in practice as a region of Croatia, and Croat representatives withdraw from Bosnian presidency and government. Despite their "parliament"'s reservations, Serbs accept plan, which requires returning 20 percent of Bosnian territory to Muslims. But they oppose any renegotiation. Bosnian army takes offensive in central Bosnia against former Croat allies.

**September 16:** Bosnian president and speaker of Bosnian Serb "parliament" sign joint declaration, providing that three republics of future "Bosnian Union" be able to secede by simple referendum after two years.

**September 22:** Croats agree to give Muslims access to sea at Neum and a concession in part of the port in Ploce. Serb officers' uprising in Banja Luka (in the self-declared Bosnian "Serb Republic") against corruption.

**September 27:** Vojislav Seselj's followers in the Serb ultranationalist Radical Party submit motion of censure against Serbian government.

**September 30:** Alliance between Serbian President Milosevic and Seselj is broken. Milosevic's Socialist Party denounces "war crimes" committed by Seselj's militias in Croatia and Bosnia. Croatian opposition and Catholic Church, uneasy about central Bosnian Croats' fate and risks of losing Serb-controlled Krajina, increasingly challenge Franjo Tudjman's and Mate Boban's policies in Bosnia.

**October 4:** Armed clashes in Bihac enclave, unilaterally declared autonomous region in northwestern Bosnia, between forces supporting provincial leader Fikret Abdic and troops loyal to President Izetbegovic.

**October 22:** Fikret Abdic signs agreement with Bosnian Serb and Croat leaders Karadzic and Boban.

**October 25:** Following death of Danish driver in central Bosnia, given humanitarian aid convoys' increasing insecurity, UNHCR decides to suspend convoys. Thousands of people receive no aid for over a month.

**November 2:** Bosnian Army Chief of Staff Sefer Halilovic is ousted, accused of having covered up "war crimes."

**November 16:** Destruction of old Mostar bridge and entire old Muslim city by Croat forces: a profound cultural and human disaster. Serbs and Muslims around Mostar begin to ally against Croats.

**December 19:** Legislative elections in Serbia: Milosevic's Socialist Party gains, but falls two votes short of parliamentary majority; democratic opposition loses five seats; Vojislav Seselj's Radical Party, no longer allied with Milosevic, loses heavily; Serb militia leader "Arkan" is not reelected in Kosovo.

**December 22:** Meeting in Brussels fails, except for joint declarations by Presidents Milosevic and Tudjman over Croatian Serb Krajina.

**December 25:** Christmas truce is not respected. Bombing of Sarajevo, whose partition is demanded by Serbs, intensifies. Radovan Karadzic opposes reopening of Tuzla airport. Muslim offensive against Croat HVO forces continues in central Bosnia.

**1994  January:** British General Rose replaces Belgian General Briquemont as head of UNPROFOR in Bosnia.

**January 11:** NATO summit in Brussels decides to reopen Tuzla airport.

**February 3:** UN Security Council threatens Croatia with economic sanctions for its role in Bosnian war.

**February 5:** Mortar shell kills sixty-eight and wounds almost 200 in Sarajevo market: the worst massacre since siege of Sarajevo began in April 1992.

**February 9:** Bosnian Serbs sign ceasefire accord with Bosnian Muslims. NATO demands that Serbs withdraw heavy weapons from Sarajevo heights by February 21, threatening air strikes in response to attacks on civilian targets. Controls over Bosnian weapons are also foreseen.

**February 16:** Greece begins embargo against former Yugoslav Macedonia.

**February 18:** Russian envoy Vitaly Churkin announces success of his diplomatic mission to Serbs. Karadzic announces withdrawal of heavy weapons from Sarajevo on condition of arrival of Russian UN forces.

**February 20-21:** Noting Serbs' turnover of 225 pieces of heavy artillery and withdrawal of equivalent number of weapons, NATO and UN announce no air strikes "at this stage" but say ultimatum still holds.

**February 25:** UN ceasefire agreement in Zagreb between Croats and Bosnian forces.

**February-March:** Meeting in Sarajevo of Bosnian Serbs opposed to Greater Serbia in presence of US and Russian envoys.

**March:** Washington Accords form a Bosnian Muslim-Croat federation and propose a confederation with Croatia.

**March 7:** UNPROFOR Nordic Battalion takes control of Tuzla airport. While truce is more or less respected in Sarajevo, Serb forces take offensive against Maglaj and Bihac enclave. Withdrawal of Croat heavy weapons from Mostar begins. Seven hundred demonstrate in Sarajevo against partition of their city.

**May:** New "contact group" (France, Britain, Germany, United States, and Russia) proposes dividing Bosnia between Croat-Muslim federation (51 percent) and Serbs (49 percent, which implies return of about 20 percent of Bosnian territory without either recognition or contiguity for "Serb Republic"). Croat-Muslim federation accepts it despite reservations. Milosevic says he will accept it. Bosnian Serbs reject it, demanding recognition and right to join Serbia.

**August:** Bosnian Army offensives, particularly in Muslim Bihac enclave against Fikret Abdic's autonomist forces. Offensive continues against Serb forces.

**Fall-Winter:** Serb counteroffensive, aided by Fikret Abdic's forces and forces coming from Croatian Serb Krajina. Siege of Bihac. Defeat of Bosnian Army's Fifth Corps. France proposes allowing Bosnian Serbs the right to confederate with Serbia. Jimmy Carter's mediation in Sarajevo leads to four-month ceasefire agreement, to begin January 1995, signed by Bosnian representatives and Radovan Karadzic. Bosnia demands Krajina Serbs' withdrawal from Bihac enclave.

# Notes

## Introduction. The Yugoslav Crisis: An Overview

1. The official name of the country formed in 1918 was "the Kingdom of Serbs, Croats, and Slovenes." It was renamed Yugoslavia in 1929. *Yugo* means "south," so *Yugoslav* means "South Slav." But not all South Slavs are Yugoslavs: Bulgarians are also South Slavs.
2. See the chronological appendix. Besides the works cited in the bibliography, see Yvan Djuric, "Les racines historiques du conflit serbo-croate," *Etudes*, October 1991, pp. 293-303.
3. Rada Ivekovic, "La libanisation de la balkanisation" and "Folies balkaniques," in *Migrations Littéraires*, no. 18/19, special issue on "Le séisme yougoslave" (Fall/Winter 1991/1992): 91-94.
4. Xavier Gautier, *L'Europe à l'Épreuve des Balkans*, pp. 28-29. Complete references for works cited will be found in the bibliography at the end of the book.
5. "Le miroir serbe," *Libération*, 29 June 1993.
6. See the Rijeka Democratic Forum's report on culture and education in Croatia, 31 October 1993.
7. Croat and Serb grammarians put together the common basis of the Serbo-Croatian language 150 years ago. The other Slavic languages of ex-Yugoslavia are Macedonian, which was established as an official language under Tito's regime, and Slovene.
8. Besides the bibliography on this subject, see "Le débat franco-allemand," *Le Monde*, 3 July 1993.
9. See the Rijeka Democratic Forum's report on citizenship, 31 October 1993.
10. For many years, people could not call themselves "Yugoslav" in the census. This word referred to the citizenship (affiliation with the Yugoslav state) that everyone shared, but not to a "nationality" (in the ethnic-cultural sense) that any one person could choose. Rejection of the "unitary" character of the first (pre-World War II) Yugoslavia, which attempted to impose a Yugoslav nationality on everyone, contributed to a suspicion of any cultural or "ethnic" "Yugoslavism," which was seen as a threat to particular identities. But people could tell the census-taker that they were

"undetermined," which is what more than 1.2 million "Yugoslavs" did in 1981: 7.9 percent in Bosnia, 8.2 percent in Croatia, 0.7 percent in Macedonia, 5.3 percent in Montenegro, 4.7 percent in Serbia—but 8.2 percent in Voivodina and 0 percent in Kosovo— and 1.3 percent in Slovenia.
11. In Serbo-Croatian and in French, *muslim* with a small "m" refers to religion. With a capital "M," *Muslim* refers to a national community, which was recognized in the 1960s under Tito and in the 1974 constitution.
12. Joseph Krulic, *Histoire de la Yougoslavie*, p. 209.
13. See the bibliography's section on national questions, particularly Alain Gresh's *Les nationalismes contre la démocratie?*
14. Krulic, *Histoire*, p. 117.
15. Bernard Féron, "Yougoslavie, origines d'un conflit," p. 89.
16. See Catherine Samary, *Le marché contre l'autogestion— L'experience yougoslave.*
17. See bibliography.
18. See Catherine Samary, "Dossier réfugiés" on ex-Yugoslavia, *Le Monde diplomatique*, January 1994.

## 1. Indeterminate Nationalities

1. The use of "Kosovo" rather than the Albanian "Kosove" is not meant to imply that this province "belongs" to Serbia. In any event, Serbs call it "Kosovo-Metohija": the second name, of Greek origin, refers to a monastery and serves as a reminder of the importance of Orthodox monastic lands in the Middle Ages. "Kosovo" was the name used when the province enjoyed the most autonomy, under the 1974 constitution, and is still the name most commonly used.
2. Joseph Krulic, *Histoire de la Yougoslavie*, p. 137.
3. Michel Roux, *Les Albanais en Yougoslavie*, p. 21.
4. On recent conflicts in Kosovo see particularly Krulic (pp. 133-42), Branka Magas' *The Destruction of Yugoslavia*, and Michel Roux.
5. Michel Roux, "Guerre civile et enjeux territoriaux en Yougoslavie," *Hérodote* no. 63, pp. 14-40.
6. We will not go into the enormous semantic debates. The word *people* or *nation* is used, as in Yugoslav tradition, to refer to an ethnic and cultural community that either has a country or demands one. *Ethnic group* is a broader category, for groups that have common characteristics (religion, language, culture, history, etc.) apart from any political territorialization. No reference is intended to the idea of "race" that was once often associated with the idea of ethnicity.
7. See particularly the magazine *L'aventure humaine* (Paris) and the works and essays of Dobrica Cosic, writer and former president of the Yugoslav (Serbo-Montengrin) Federation.

8. "The oppressor's religion" refers to Islam for the Serbs ruled by the Ottoman empire, Catholicism for those who, because of migrations or international boundary shifts, found themselves under Austro-Hungarian rule.
9. Macedonia was conquered by the Greeks, Bulgarians, and/or Serbs in succession (each conqueror tending to "take over the nationality" along with the territory). The Macedonian language is close to Bulgarian. The area was partitioned in the end between Greece, Bulgaria, and Yugoslavia.
10. See Christophe Chiclet, "Etouffement de la Macédoine," *Le Monde diplomatique*, September 1992, reprinted in *Manière de Voir*, no. 17, pp. 60-61.
11. See Catherine Lutard, "Le Monténégro est-il une nation?," *Le Monde diplomatique*, June 1992, reprinted in *Manière de voir*, no. 17, pp. 58-59.
12. On Islam in the Balkans see the interview with Alexander Popovic published in *Quantara*, January-March 1993, pp. 19-22.
13. Paul Garde, *Vie et mort de la Yougoslavie*, p. 188, denies this, without denying the existence of a Bosnian heresy.
14. The Bosnian converts were the ancestors of the nationality whose members are called "Muslims" today.
15. Reprinted in the collection *Titanic et autres contes juifs*, pp. 75-92. Reading Andric's works can be extraordinarily helpful in conveying what Bosnia was like under the Ottoman empire (in the case of *The Bridge on the Drina* [Chicago: University of Chicago Press, 1977]) or during the transition to Austro-Hungarian rule (in the case of *Bosnian Chronicle* [New York: Arcade, 1993]).
16. See Cedomir Nestorovic's article "Bosnie-Herzégovine" in *Encyclopédie de l'Europe* (Paris: Seuil, 1993), pp. 49-54.
17. Many of the Jews fleeing from Isabella the Catholic's persecutions in fifteenth century Spain took refuge in the Turkish empire, particularly in Sarajevo.
18. Thus the Serbs under Ottoman rule had their own Orthodox patriarchate in Pec in Kosovo in the middle of the sixteenth century.
19. Xavier Bougarel, "Bon voisinage et crime intime, à propos de la guere en Bosnie-Herzégovine," *Confluences Méditerranée*, January 1995. For a picture of Bosnian society see also Robert J. Donia's and John V.A. Fine Jr.'s remarkable book, *Bosnia and Herzegovina: A Tradition Betrayed*.
20. Nenad Fiser, "Tout ce que vous vouliez savoir sur la guerre en Bosnie—petit manuel pour faire la guerre (et s'en débarrasser)," *Lignes*, no. 20, pp. 45-58.
21. Fiser, ibid., p. 53.
22. The official terminology has changed in Bosnia, and been codified in the constitution of the new Croat-Muslim federation. The term

*Muslim* now refers only to religion. A member of the Muslim ethnic-national community is now called a *Bosnjak* (pronounced "Boshnyak")—as distinct from *Bosanac*, which refers to a citizen of Bosnia in general. Using the word *Bosnjak* has the advantage of avoiding the ambiguity of the word *Muslim*. But it also reflects the rise of a "*Bosnjak* nationalism" that defines Bosnia as only the Muslim community's country. The exact connotation of these words will be made clear in political practice.

23. See Midhat Begic, *La Bosnie, carrefour d'identités culturelles*, particularly the chapter, "L'écrivain musulman dans les lettres yougoslaves," pp. 15-27.
24. See *Migration Littéraire*, no. 18-19, special issue on "Le séisme yougoslave" (Fall-Winter 1991-1992): 56-64.
25. Lecture given by Professor Stanoje Stanojevic of the University of Belgrade at the Geographical Society in 1918, reprinted in *Migrations Littéraires*, ibid.
26. See Paul Garde, *Vie et mort de la Yougoslavie*, p. 50.
27. Joseph Krulic, *Histoire de la Yougoslavie*, pp. 25-26.
28. Bernard Féron, *Yougoslavie: Origines d'un Conflit*, p. 26.
29. "L'intelligentsia dans l'autre Europe," *Lignes*, no. 20, pp. 141-54.
30. The Ustashe ("rebels") were Croat fascist groups led by Ante Pavelic. Note: Sometimes the Serbo-Croat grammatical forms are used in English: one *Ustashe*, two *Ustasha*.
31. The first Chetniks were Serb resistance groups formed at the beginning of the twentieth century. The name was borrowed during World War II by Serb troops led by General Draza Mihajlovic, who were supposed to fight against the German and Italian occupiers on behalf of the former Yugoslav regime (whose Serb royal family had fled to London). These latter-day Chetniks often compromised their resistance to fascism in order to attack the Communists.
32. See in particular Anton Ciliga (1974).
33. Milosevic allied himself after 1986 with Vojislav Seselj's Radical Party, whose militias played an essential role in building Greater Serbia. Vuk Draskovic, leader of the Serbian Renewal Party, laid claim to the same Chetnik tradition and the goal of Greater Serbia before breaking with Seselj in order to oppose Milosevic. Milosevic decided in September 1993 to "discover" and punish the crimes committed by his former ally Seselj when Seselj seemed to him more dangerous than useful to the Serbian government.

## 2. Titoism's Balance Sheet

1. See the *Memorandum of the Serbian Academy of Sciences*, whose entire text was reprinted in French in *Dialogue* no. 2/3 (September 1992). This chapter is based on a previously published article:

"L'éclatement yougoslave, un cas à part?," *La Pensée*, no. 296 (November-December 1993), pp. 15-22.
2. See Franjo Tudjman's speech of 30 May 1991 (on the eve of the Croatian declaration of independence), published in French in *Review of International Affairs* (Belgrade), no. 989 (20 June 1991): 13.
3. See the *Memorandum*, p. 19.
4. The disagreements between economists Kosta Mihailovic and Branko Horvat are analyzed in Catherine Samary, *Le marché contre l'autogestion*, particularly in part 2, pp. 125-27.
5. This nationalist movement was often called the "Croatian Spring" by analogy to the 1968 "Prague Spring." Like the Prague Spring, it was largely pushed forward by a reform wing of the Communist Party (led by Mika Tripalo and Savka-Dabcevic Kucar) that was subsequently "purged." While it had cultural dimensions (demanding freedom to use Croat dialects of Serbo-Croatian), its main demands were political and economic. It argued against the powers retained by the central government, for example over the currency. Unlike the Prague Spring it took place not at the beginning of market reforms but six years later; and the Yugoslav market reforms were more radical than anything proposed by Czechoslovak reformers. The Croatian movement that demanded a still greater decentralization in favor of the republics developed at the same time as growing workers' strikes on a non-nationalist basis, particularly in Slovenia and Croatia, against the reforms' inequitable effects. The intelligentsia and student groups were divided by these movements. The Catholic Church and the Croat nationalist organization *Matitsa Hrvatska* supported the Croatian Spring, as did Croat emigrants in other countries and peasant groups.
6. The Social Product was used in Yugoslavia and other so-called socialist countries as a more restrictive version of GNP: it depends on an evaluation of a country's production of goods: services are included only if they contribute directly to production of goods.
7. Only Slovenia and Croatia had per capita Social Products above the Yugoslav average (respectively 121 percent and 28 percent above the average). See *Courier des Pays de l'Est*, November 1991.
8. *Courier des Pays de l'Est*, November 1991.
9. Political tensions grew up at the end of the 1980s, particularly when peace movements denounced threats that the Yugoslav army would intervene in Slovenia. One young peace activist, Janez Jansa, one of the founders of the magazine *Mladina*, was tried before a military court. He later became defense minister of independent Slovenia.
10. See Cedomir Nestorovic's article in Edith Lhomel and Thomas Schreiber, eds., *L'Europe Centrale et Orientale en 1991*, Documentation française, p. 231.

11. Similar arguments and later similar disillusionment existed in the USSR. The richer Soviet republics thought at first that they were exploited by the Russian center. Only after the USSR's collapse were they brutally confronted with the reality of world energy and raw material prices and the difficulty of exporting in face of the rise of protectionism, particularly in Western Europe.
12. On Slovenia's situation after independence, see Catherine Samary, *Manière de Voir*, no. 17 (February 1993).
13. The CPY had nonetheless been one of the strongest Communist parties in Eastern Europe immediately after the 1917 Russian Revolution, with impressive electoral results in the new country's industrial cities and a decisive influence in the trade unions. But its banning and the persecution of its members underground combined with problems of political orientation, internal disagreements, and factional settling of accounts in the worst Stalinist tradition, all of which explain its decline in the interwar years.
14. See the accounts by Dedijer, Djilas, Fejtö, Maurer, and Pijade listed in the bibliography.
15. François Fejtö, *Histoire des Democraties Populaires: L'Ere de Staline*, pp. 196-200.
16. Enver Hoxha's Albania preferred its more distant Soviet big brother to its omnipresent Yugoslav big brother during the Tito-Stalin conflict.
17. Rastko Mocnik, "Trois mythes et une hypothèse," *Migrations Littéraires*, no. 18-19 (Fall-Winter 1991/1992), pp. 68-76.
18. There is also a substantial Albanian minority in Montenegro, and Albanians make up more than 20 percent of the population in Macedonia. (Albanians estimate that today, with the flight of Albanians from Kosovo, they are 40 percent of the population in Macedonia.) The educational opportunities in Albanian in Macedonia were lower than in the autonomous province.
19. See Catherine Samary (1988).
20. Branko Horvat, "Les caprices de l'économie," *Peuples Méditerranéens*, no. 61 (October-December 1992): 13, 11.
21. The Agrokomerk scandal in Bosnia-Herzegovina not only discredited its chief executive officer Fikret Abdic (who later headed the secessionist statelet in the Bihac area of Bosnia), but also led to the resignation of Serbian leader Ivan Stambolic.
22. Vukovar was a Croatian town typical of the Yugoslav mix: during the war in Croatia it became a martyred city, laid siege to and largely destroyed by the Serb forces' artillery. According to the Croatian opposition, President Tudjman was complicit in the town's destruction in keeping with his partition agreements with Milosevic.
23. Contrary to his prevalent image, however, Milosevic was no more hostile to the market and privatizations than his colleagues at

the head of other Yugoslav republics or East bloc countries. Like that of the others, his economic rhetoric and practice would evolve; as with the others, his promises of social protection came to the fore at election time and during open social conflicts. The aspect of his government that looks backward toward the Serbian past is also composite and evolving: it involves a break with Titoism and an alliance with traditionally anticommunist nationalist currents, in spite of the official references to socialism.

24. In the first pluralist elections in Serbia in December 1990, the ex-Communists won 194 out of 250 seats in parliament and Milosevic himself won 65 percent of the vote.
25. The aid was spent largely on prestige investments or on technology that was not labor-intensive, despite the fact that the province had a mushrooming population. But it is one thing to criticize mismanagement and another thing to describe the province as a mere "colony," which it was not. During the 1970s it received the bulk of Development Fund investments and enjoyed a remarkable cultural development, including an Albanian-language university—although Albanian women were shut out of this process. See in particular Michel Roux, *Les Albanais en Yougoslavie*.
26. These allegations were never confirmed. Investigations of rape showed that Serb women were raped proportionately as often by Serb men as by Albanian men; but then Serb-on-Serb rape was presumably considered to be "normal." Serb flight from the province was a reality, as were the tensions between the two communities that did not intermingle. But demographic and socioeconomic pressures played an important role in the Serb exodus. The typically "Titoist" method of dealing with tensions—silencing expressions of hostility rather than encouraging public discussion—also contributed to the crisis.
27. The Titoist regime was always good at exploiting the Soviet threat, including the 1968 intervention in Czechoslovakia that was hardly a threat for Yugoslavia. At that time a "territorial defense" was created in each republic, a popular citizen army alongside the official army. The weapons that were used for regular training were thus spread throughout the whole country.

## 3. Wars Within the War

1. See in particular Mirjana Morokvasic, "Logique de l'exclusion," *Peuples Méditerranéans*, no. 61, pp. 279-93.
2. See Joze Mencinger (Slovenian economist and minister in the government formed after the 1990 elections), "Emergency exit," *Balkan War Report*, December 1994/January 1995.
3. *Review of International Affairs* (Belgrade), no. 989 (20 June 1991), gives the standpoint of all the protagonists (Ante Markovic and

the various republican governments) on how the crisis should be settled.
4. This last phrase is a judgment made by Svetlana Slapsak, a "bad Serb" academic who was put on trial in 1988 for having dared to call for the release of Albanian political prisoner Adem Demaci. See "Les alternatives serbes: y en a-t-il après la Bosnie?," *Migrations Littéraires*, no. 21 (Summer 1992): 3-17.
5. This is the main contradiction in which the Belgrade and Zagreb governments are caught as they persist in their policy of dismembering Bosnia-Herzegovina. They have been able and will be able on occasion to dissociate themselves from the warlords running the self-proclaimed republics and from those warlords' crimes, as long as they think that this is in the best interests of their own power.
6. Yvan Djuric, "Serbes et Croates—que faut-il faire maintenant?," *Lignes*, no. 20 (September 1993): 14-30.
7. Without daring to say so in public, some people in Slovenia even think, as Ivan Djuric's remarks suggest, that this was the Serbian and Slovenian leaders' real, covert aim.
8. See *Review of International Affairs*, no. 989 (20 June 1991).
9. In this case the frontiers were Yugoslavia's, not Slovenia's.
10. The transition from a Titoist to a Greater Serbian project is undoubtedly difficult to date: the crisis affecting Yugoslav society and its institutions also necessarily cut through the army. In each nationality there are examples of officers who rallied to "their" national cause and of others who remained committed for various reasons (not only material interests) to a Yugoslav cause. Of course a Yugoslav cause could ensure Serb domination, as in the first Yugoslavia. Some of the Serb officers and general staff certainly worked consciously for the achievement of a Greater Serbian project from the late 1980s on.
11. Slobodan Milosevic's wife was one of the founding members of this Party of Yugoslav Communists.
12. The eighth session of the central committee of the League of Serbian Communists in September 1987 was when Milosevic became political leader of Serbia.
13. Branko Horvat, *Peuples Méditerranéens*, no. 61, p. 23. A Croat economist, Horvat was one of the founding members of the Union for a Yugoslav Democratic Initiative, which defended the rights of Kosovo Albanians in the late 1980s. Today he is one of the leaders of the Social-Democratic Union of Croatia.
14. This is what the soldiers said, as recorded on the cassette "Ljubljana Under the Barricades." The cassette was sold proudly in the streets of the Slovenian capital, in the midst of the nationalist, martial atmosphere that surrounded this whole episode.

15. This was part of the Titoist legacy of a decentralized force parallel to the official army, in which the old Partisan tradition played a certain role. It dated back to 1968, after the Soviet intervention in Czechoslovakia, and was meant to maintain popular mobilization in each republic against "foreign or domestic threats." Regular exercises and popular mobilizations went together with decentralized distribution of weapons to local barracks. The Yugoslav army responded to the crisis by beginning to recentralize weapons in the various republics. Slovenia resisted this process.

16. A Serbian-American businessman, Milan Panic was seen as a simple, powerless pawn of Milosevic when he was named Yugoslav prime minister in July 1992. But he won support among the democratic opposition, particularly among young people who were tired of war, by giving speeches about peace—which Milosevic would plagiarize later, after having ousted him. Panic challenged Milosevic by running against him for president of Serbia in the December 1992 elections. Part of the army, more interested in consolidating its privileges by gaining international recognition for the new Yugoslav (Serbian-Montenegrin) federation than in supporting Greater Serbia, visibly leaned toward Panic for a while in hopes that he would bring about an end to the war and lifting of the sanctions. But Milosevic succeeded in defeating Panic, and soon afterwards ousted him as Yugoslav prime minister.

17. "L'état des oppositions démocratiques en ex-Yougoslavie," *La Nouvelle Alternative*, no. 30 (June 1993): 8-11. See also Catherine Lutard's articles in *Diagonale Est/Ouest* (Lyon), July 1993, pp. 26-28, and in *Le Monde diplomatique*, July 1993, p. 14.

18. *The Guardian*, 18 November 1993, p. 4.

19. Branko Horvat, *Peuples Méditerranéens*, no. 61, p. 22.

20. Milorad Pupovac, "Les Serbes pris dans l'étau," in ibid., p. 149.

21. In Russia as well, World War II continues to influence the ideology of the so-called "red-brown" alliance: in this case it is the neo-Stalinists who claim the heritage of the antifascist struggle.

22. "Arkan" is a pseudonym used by the Serb mercenary Zeljko Raznjatovic, who worked for the secret police under the old regime.

23. See Catherine Humblot, "Ex-Yougoslavie: médias fauteurs de guerre," *Le Monde*, 22-25 July 1993, and *Reporters and Media in Ex-Yugoslavia: IJO Notebooks* (International Journalists Organization), no. 2 (January 1993).

24. See Rada Ivekovic, "Femmes, nationalisme et guerre ('Faites l'amour, pas la guerre')" and Zarana Papic, "Ex-citoyennes dans l'ex-Yougoslavie," in *Peuples Méditerranéens*, no. 61, pp. 205-15.

## 4. The Bosnian Symbol

1. Xavier Bougarel, "Bosnie-Herzégovine, anatomie d'une poudrière," *Hérodote*, no. 67 (October-December 1992): 84-148.
2. Bougarel, ibid., p. 86.
3. Bougarel distinguishes: *homogeneous* municipalities have one dominant ethnic group whose numbers exceed 80 percent of the population; in *majority-binational* municipalities, the largest group makes up 60 to 80 percent of the population and the second-largest group is more than twice as large as the third-largest group; in *balanced binational* municipalities, the two largest groups each are more than twice as large as the third-largest; in *majority-heterogeneous* municipalities, the second-largest group is less than twice as big as the third-largest; and in *balanced-heterogeneous* municipalities, no group is decisively larger than the others.
4. Bougarel, ibid., p. 101.
5. There are obviously margins of error and conflicting interpretations of statistics in a context in which the Muslim community had no official opportunity to identify as such. It could only be estimated by various measures (according to religious affiliations, people who called themselves "none of the above," etc.), which Bougarel lays out.
6. Bougarel, p. 101.
7. According to I. Bakic, cited by Bougarel, ibid., pp. 89 and 133.
8. Bougarel, ibid., p. 125.
9. Ibid., p. 132.
10. Ibid., p. 117.
11. Mirjana Morokvasik, "La guerre et les réfugiés dans l'ex-Yougoslavie," *Revue Européenne des Migrations Internationales* (Poitiers) 8, no. 2 (1992): 5-25.
12. Serbs, Croats, and Muslims are all Slavs; and we have already noted that Muslims are considered Serbs by Serb nationalists and considered Croats by Croat nationalists.
13. Fiser, "Tout ce que vous vouliez savoir sur la Bosnie-Herzégovine...." *Lignes*, no. 20, p. 50.
14. Fiser, ibid.
15. In the last months of Serb-dominated Yugoslavia, a Serb-Croat agreement in 1939 established a "Croatian Banovina" that included part of Bosnia-Herzegovina, while the rest of Bosnia remained under Serbo-Yugoslav domination. See the analysis made by Philippe Koulisher from the association "Mirna Bosna" in Geneva, published in *Inprecor*, no. 370 (June 1993): 4-6.
16. Xavier Bougarel, "Etat et communautarisme en Bosnie-Herzégovine," *Cultures et Conflits*, no. 13 (December 1994).
17. See *Livre noir de l'ex-Yougoslavie: Purification ethnique et crimes de guerre* (Paris, 1993), pp. 54-55.

18. The HDZ's rephrasing of the referendum question was reprinted in *Borba*, 10 February 1992. On these episodes and Bosnia-Herzegovina's political evolution, see in particular Xavier Bougarel, "Etat et communautarisme en Bosnie-Herzégovine."
19. Many of these Bosnians often speak of "urbicide" in order to describe the political strategy of destroying a civilization by laying siege to its cities, where the civilization is crystallized.
20. Bogdan Useljenicki, "Izetbegovic contre la Bosnie?," *Libération*, 8 November 1993, p. 5.
21. Reprinted as an appendix to Samary, *The Fragmentation of Yugoslavia*, pp. 45-46.
22. This text, along with the Serbian Memorandum already mentioned and extracts from Franjo Tudjman's last book, can be found in *Revue Dialogue*, no. 2/3 (September 1992).
23. The Arab world has been astonished to discover these "Muslims," many of whom know hardly anything about Islam and do not observe its precepts. However, as the Muslim community is isolated and massacred, as refugees from the villages are massively displaced toward the cities, as less urbanized Muslim refugees from the Serbian Sanjak arrive in Bosnia, and as a "Muslim country" is created from enclaves cut off from the world, fundamentalist influence can only flourish.
24. *Libération*, 20 October 1993.
25. For the "Lebanonization" of the war and the warlords' importance and relative autonomy among both Serbs and Croats, see also Xavier Gautier, *L'Europe à l'épreuve des Balkans*, pp. 81-89.
26. In his book *Mordet Pa Sarayevo* (published in Denmark in 1993), Zelko Vukovic discusses these conflicts openly. Vukovic fled from Sarajevo in 1992 in order to take refuge in Norway.
27. *Libération*, 8 September 1993.
28. "Le funeste plan de paix pour la Bosnie," *Libération*, 20 October 1993.
29. See Catherine Samary, "Tuzla sous pression," *Le Monde diplomatique*, December 1994.
30. Clearly, the arms embargo has hurt only the Bosnian forces.
31. Useljenicki, *Libération*, 8 November 1993.
32. See Catherine Samary, "Sans patrie ni frontières—l'odyssée des réfugiés de l'ex-Yougoslavie" and "Les murailles toujours plus élevées de la forteresse Europe," *Le Monde diplomatique*, January 1994, pp. 10-11.
33. Midhat Begic, *La Bosnie, carrefour d'identités culturelles*, pp. 15-27.
34. See Catherine Samary, "Les incertitudes de la Fédération croato-musulmane," *Le Monde diplomatique*, June 1994.
35. See "La question Serbe et la question allemande," *Hérodote*, no. 67 (October-December 1992): 3-49.

36. *Les vérités yougoslaves ne sont pas toutes bonnes à dire*, p. 202.
37. Interview with Ambassador Gabriel Robin, *Le Figaro*, 16 July 1993.

## 5. The "International Community" On Trial

1. See in the bibliography: X. Gautier, J. Rupnik, *Cahiers du Crest, Dossiers du Grip, Hérodote*. See also the different viewpoints expressed in the *Balkan War Report* special issue on "The UN's War" (September 1994) as well as its December 1994/January 1995 issue; Paul-Marie de la Gorce, "Coûteuse myopie des grandes puissances," *Le Monde diplomatique*, July 1992, reprinted in *Manière de Voir*, no. 17, pp. 35-39; de la Gorce, "Les occasions manquées," *Le Monde diplomatique*, November 1994; and (for a different point of view) Antoine Sanguinetti, "Faux fuyants européens," *Le Monde diplomatique*, January 1995.
2. On the first identification, see my study, *Plan, Market, and Democracy: The Experience of the So-Called Socialist Countries*; on the second, see my contribution to the seminars organized on the theme *Paradigms of Democracy*, Jacques Bidet, ed. (Paris: Presses Universitaires de France, 1994).
3. Samary, *Plan, Market, and Democracy*. Joseph Krulic, in *Histoire de la Yougoslavie*, points to the uncritical blindness of these left-wing currents, but fails to mention that another approach to the Yugoslav experience is possible, an approach that would criticize the Titoist political and economic system *from a pro-self-management standpoint*. If no critical evaluation is made, then any attempt to find a third way is simply buried on the basis of the crisis of one specific experience.
4. See Catherine Samary, "Eastern Europe and the former USSR five years on: economic reform in the East," *International Viewpoint*, no. 264 (March 1995): 18-23.
5. After the death of a Danish UN soldier, it was decided to break off humanitarian convoys in Bosnia, leaving the starving Bosnian population without any help for several months during the fall of 1993.
6. By contrast, the Badinter Commission considered the guarantees offered to minorities sufficient to justify recognizing Macedonia—but a European Union veto by Greece slowed down the process. Greece considered that the name "Macedonia" was its exclusive property, and that its use by an independent country was in itself a threat to Greece's territorial integrity. Historic Macedonia was divided by Balkan wars and treaties in 1912 to 1920 between Greece, Bulgaria, and Serbia (which then became part of the first Yugoslavia). Considered "South Serbia" by Serb nationalists, Macedonia was recognized in Tito's Yugoslavia as one of its constituent republics, with its own official language. This consol-

idated a "Macedonian nation." After the break-up of Yugoslavia, Macedonian independence has been recognized by Bulgaria (though Bulgaria considers Macedonia as a second country within the *Bulgarian* nation). Greece, by contrast, has imposed a boycott of Macedonia, which is also experiencing major tensions with its Albanian minority (20 percent of its population, not counting the many Albanians who have fled from repression in Kosovo).
7. The Serbian government's question was: "Do the Serb populations of Croatia and Bosnia-Herzegovina, as one of the constituent nations of Yugoslavia, enjoy the right to self-determination?"
8. *Avis*, no. 2 (11 January 1992).
9. All of the "peoples" in the area *are* minorities, since there is no absolute majority in Bosnia-Herzegovina.
10. See *Balkan War Report*, April/May 1993.
11. Ibid.
12. On this subject see Cedomir Nestorovic, "Le droit des peuples à disposer d'eux-mêmes et la crise yougoslave," *Relations Internationales et Stratégiques*, Summer 1992, pp. 29-42; Nestorovic, "Question nationale ou question constitutionnelle?," *Cosmopolitiques*, February 1991, pp. 12-20; *Nouvelle Europe*, nos. 5 & 6, particularly Nestorovic, "La médiation européenne en Yougoslavie: chronologie d'un échec," pp. 38-42.
13. *Libération*, 20 October 1993.

### Conclusion. Today Yugoslavia; Tomorrow Europe?

1. Tibor Varady, "Les minorités: sources de crise et clés du dénouement," *Migrations Littéraires*, Fall/Winter 1991-1992, pp. 46-50. See also Drejan Janjic, "Les minorités entre absence de droit et démocratie," *Peuples Méditerranéens*, no. 61, pp. 271-79.
2. Rada Ivekovic, *Migrations Littéraires*, no. 18-19, p. 91.
3. See the collection edited by Alain Gresh, *A l'Est: Les Nationalismes contre la Démocratie?*
4. The Universal Declaration of the Collective Rights of Peoples, adopted in 1990 by the European Conference of Stateless Nations, upholds every people's right to define itself "as a nation" whenever its members express the "will to organize themselves politically."
5. See Boris Vukobrat et al., *Towards a New Community* (Zug/Belgrade: Peace and Crises Management Foundation, 1992).
6. See the bibliography.
7. Document from the Hungarian Ministry of Foreign Affairs, Budapest, 1994. It should be noted that there are no substantial Romanian or Slovak minorities left in Hungary today. When Hungary did have large minorities, before 1918, its policies aimed at forcing them to assimilate.

8. The struggle for diversity and against ghettoes justifies great efforts to encourage people, from childhood on, to learn several languages: national languages, mother tongues, and languages that are used more widely, internationally.
9. Michel Wievorka, *La démocratie à l'épreuve, Nationalisme, populisme, ethnicité.*
10. Joint declaration in Chiapas by Mexican Indian organizations, 8 November 1994 (translated from Spanish).
11. See Michael Löwy, "Why nationalism," *Socialist Register* (London), no. 29 (1993), pp. 125-38.
12. This expressive phrase is used in ex-Czechoslavakia to describe the Czech nationalist aim of "dumping" the burden of Slovakia. The expression can be generalized to describe the "dumping" of Yugoslavia by its richer regions, Slovenia and Croatia, and similar phenomena in other parts of Europe.
13. See Catherine Samary, "Choc sans thérapie," *Diagonales Est-Ouest*, Summer 1992, pp. 13-16; and "Les fragilités sociales à l'Est," *Diagonales Est-Ouest*, October 1993, pp. 6-13.
14. Predrag Matvejevic, "L'intelligentsia dans l'autre Europe," *Lignes*, no. 20, pp. 141-53.

# BIBLIOGRAPHY

## BOOKS AND BROCHURES

### On Yugoslavia

Andric, Ivo. *Titanic et autres contes juifs*. Paris: Ed. Belfond, 1987.
Auty, Phyllis. *Tito: A Biography*. London: Longman, 1970.
Begic, Midhat. *La Bosnie: Carrefour d'identité culturelle*. Paris: L'Esprit des Péninsules, 1994.
Ciliga, Anton. *Crise d'Etat dans la Yougoslavie de Tito*. Paris: Denoël, 1974.
Cosic, Dobrica. *La Yougoslavie et la question serbe*. Lausanne: L'Age d'Homme, 1992.
Crnobrnja, Mihailo. *The Yugoslav Drama*. London: Tauris, 1994.
Dedijer, Vladimir. *The Battle Stalin Lost*. New York: Viking Press, 1971.
Denitch, Bogdan. *Ethnic Nationalism: The Tragic Death of Yugoslavia*. Minneapolis: University of Minnesota Press, 1994.
Djilas, Milovan. *Wartime: With Tito and the Partisans*. London: Secker & Warburg, 1977.
—. *Conversations with Stalin*. New York: Harcourt Brace Jovanovich, 1962.
—. *On New Roads of Socialism*. Belgrade: Jugoslovenska knjiga, 1950.
Donia, Robert J. and John V.A. Fine Jr. *Bosnia and Herzegovina: A Tradition Betrayed*. London: Hurst & Co., 1994.
Drulovic, Milojko. *L'autogestion à l'épreuve*. Paris: Fayard, 1973.
Fejtö, François. *History of the People's Democracies*. Harmondsworth: Penguin, 1974.
Féron, Bernard. *Yougoslavie: Origines d'un conflit*. Paris: Le Monde Ed./Marabout, 1993.
Garde, Paul. *Vie et mort de la Yougoslavie*. Paris: Fayard, 1992.
Gautier, Xavier. *L'Europe à l'épreuve des Balkans*. Paris: Ed. Jacques Bertoin, 1992.
Grmek, Mirko, Marc Gjidara, and Simac Never. *Le nettoyage ethnique: Documents historiques sur une idéologie serbe*. Paris: Fayard, 1993.

Horvat, Branko. *An Essay on Yugoslav Society*. New York: International Art and Science Press, 1969.
Ivic, Pavle et al. *De l'imprécision à la falsification: Analyses de* Vie et mort de la Yougoslavie *de Paul Garde*. Lausanne: Editions l'Age d'Homme, 1992.
Julliard, Jacques. *Ce fascisme qui vient*. Paris: Seuil, 1993.
Krulic, Joseph. *Histoire de la Yougoslavie de 1945 à nos jours*. Paris: Ed. Complexe, 1993.
*Livre noir de l'ex-Yougoslavie: Purification ethnique et crimes de guerre*. Paris: Ed. Arléa, 1993.
Magas, Branka. *The Destruction of Yugoslavia: Tracking the Break-Up, 1980-92*. London: Verso, 1993.
Malcolm, Noel. *Bosnia: A Short History*. London: Macmillan, 1994.
Mauer, Pierre. *La réconciliation soviéto-yougoslave—1954-1956: Illusions et désillusions de Tito*. Lausanne: Delaval, 1991.
Meister, Albert. *Socialisme et autogestion*. Paris: Seuil, 1964.
Nahoum-Grappe, Véronique, ed. *Vukovar, Sarajevo...: La guerre en ex-Yougoslavie*. Paris: Esprit, 1993.
Pijade, Mocha. *La fable de l'aide soviétique* and *Des questions litigieuses*. Belgrade: Livre yougoslave, 1949.
Pipa, A., ed. *Studies in Kosovo*. New York: Columbia University Press, 1984.
Popovic, Alexandre. *Les musulmans yougoslaves, 1945-89*. Lausanne: Editions l'Age d'Homme, 1990.
Roux, Michel. *Les Albanais en Yougoslavie: Minorité nationale, territoire et développement*. Paris: Ed. Maison des Sciences de l'Homme, 1992.
Rupnik, Jacques, ed. *De Sarajevo à Sarajevo*. Paris: Ed. Complexes, 1992.
Rusinow, Dennison. *The Yugoslav Experiment*. Berkeley: University of California Press, 1977.
Samary, Catherine. *The Fragmentation of Yugoslavia*. Amsterdam: IIRE, 1993.
—. *Plan, Market and Democracy*. Amsterdam: IIRE, 1988.
—. *Le marché contre l'autogestion: L'expérience yougoslave*. Paris: Publisud/La Brèche, 1988.
Stark, Hans. *Les Balkans: Le retour de la guerre en Europe*. Paris: IFRI-Dunod, 1993.
Supek, Rudi et al. *Etatisme et autogestion: Bilan critique du socialisme yougoslave*. Paris: Anthropos, 1973.
Taibo, Carlos and José Carlos Lechado. *Los Conflictos Yugoslavos: Una Introducción*. Madrid: Ed. Fundamentos, 1993.

Vukobrat, Boris et al. *Towards a New Community.* Zug/Belgrade: Peace and Crises Management Foundation, 1992.
Wilson, Duncan. *Tito's Yugoslavia.* Cambridge: Cambridge University Press, 1979.

### On National Questions in General

Amin, Samir. *Class and Nation: Historically and in the Current Crisis.* New York: Monthly Review Press, 1980.
Anderson, Benedict. *Imagined Communities: Reflections on the Origins and Spread of Nationalism.* London: Verso, 1991.
Balibar, Etienne and Immanuel Wallerstein. *Race, Nation, Class.* London: Verso, 1991.
Bauer, Otto. *Die Nationalitätenfrage und die Sozialdemokratie, Werkansgaße* vol. 1. Vienna: Europaverlag, 1975 (in French: *La question des nationalités et la social-démocratie,* Paris: EDI, 1988).
Bibo, Istvan. *Misère des petits Etats d'Europe de l'Est.* Paris: Albin Michel, 1993.
Canapa, Marie-Paule et al. *Paysans et nations d'Europe central et balkanique.* Paris: Maisonneuve et Larose, 1985.
Ciron, Suzanne. *L'histoire de France, autrement.* Paris: Atelier, 1992.
Fisera, Claude-Vladimir. *Les peuples slaves et le communisme de Marx à Gorbatchev.* Paris: Berg International, 1992.
Gresh, Alain, ed. *A L'Est: Les nationalismes contre la démocratie?* Paris: Ed. Complexes, 1993.
Haupt, Georges, Michael Löwy, and Claudie Weill. *Les marxistes et la question nationale, 1848-1914.* Paris: Maspero, 1969.
Hobsbawm, Eric. *Nation and Nationalism since 1780: Programme, Myth, Reality.* Cambridge: Cambridge University Press, 1990.
Iriarte José ("Bikila"). *Do the Workers Have a Country?* Amsterdam: IIRE, 1991.
Janjic, Dusan and Bosko Kavacevic, eds. *Democracy and Minority Communities.* Belgrade/Subotica: European Civic Centre for Conflicts Resolution, 1993.
Lenin, Vladimir Ilyich. "The right of nations to self-determination," *Collected Works* vol. 20. London: Lawrence & Wishart, 1972.
Liebech, André and André Reszler, eds. *L'Europe centrale et ses minorités: Vers une solution européenne?* Paris: PUF, 1993.
Löwy, Michael. "Marxism and the national question," in Robin Blackburn, ed., *Revolution and Class Struggle: A Reader in Marxist Politics.* London: Fontana, 1977.
Luxemburg, Rosa. *The National Question.* New York: Monthly Review Press, 1976.

Munk, Ronaldo. *The Difficult Dialogue.* Oxford: Oxford University Press, 1986.

Poulton, Hugh. *The Balkans: Minorities and States in Conflict.* London: Minority Rights Publications, 1991.

Renan, Ernest. *Qu'est-ce qu'une nation?* Paris: Agora, 1992.

Rosdolsky, Roman. *Engels and the "Non-Historic" Peoples: The National Question in the Revolution of 1848.* Glasgow: Critique Books, 1986.

Weill, Claudie. *L'Internationale et l'autre: Les relations interethniques dans la IIème Internationale.* Paris: Ed. Arcantère, 1987.

Wievorka, Michel. *La démocratie à l'épreuve: Nationalisme, populisme, ethnicité.* Paris: La Découverte, 1993.

## MAGAZINES

### Special Issues on National Questions or Yugoslavia

*Confluences Méditerranée*, no. 4 (Fall 1992): "Face à l'Etat, la permanence des minorités"; no. 8 (Fall 1993): "Balkans: l'implosion?"; no. 13 (Winter 1994-1995): "Bosnie."

*Dossiers du GRIP*, no. 166 (February 1992): "La Yougoslavie désintégrée,"; no. 167 (March 1992): "La politique étrangère européenne: de Maastricht à la Yougoslavie."

*Hérodote*, no. 63 (4th quarter 1991): "Balkans et balkanisation"; no. 67 (October-December 1992): "La question serbe."

*IJO (International Journalists Organisation) Notebooks*, no. 2 (December 1992): "Reporters and media in ex-Yugoslavia."

*International Viewpoint*, no. 234 (14 September 1992): "Bosnia: a war of our times."

*Labour Focus on Eastern Europe*, no. 2 (1993): special issue on Yugoslavia.

*La Pensée*, no. 296 (November-December 1993): "Ethnicité et pouvoirs."

*L'Aventure Humaine*, Winter 1989.

*L'Evénement Européen*, no. 16 (1991): "Minorités, quelles chances pour l'Europe?"

*Lignes*, no. 20 (September 1993): "Yougoslavie, penser dans la crise."

*Manière de Voir*, no. 17 (1993).

*Nouvelle Europe*, no. 5 (May 1991): "Les frontières en Europe: entre la logique de l'Etat et le droit des peuples"; no. 6 (October 1991): "L'Europe à l'épreuve du démembrement de l'URSS et de la Yougoslavie."

*Peuples Méditerranéens*, no. 61 (October-December 1992): "Yougoslavie, logiques de l'exclusion."

**Publications with ongoing analysis and information on ex-Yugoslavia**

*Balkan War Report*, 1 Auckland St., London SE11 5HU, England.
*Dialogue* (in English, French, and Serbo-Croatian), 17 Ch. du Pont d'Herville, 78520 Guernes, France.
*Kosova Communication*, Centre d'information de la République de Kosove, CP 6376, 1211 Geneva, Switzerland.
*Labour Focus on Eastern Europe*, 77 Morrell Avenue, Oxford OX4 1NQ, England.

# INDEX

Abdic, Fikret, 20, 99, 100-101, 108, 109
Agrokomerk (conglomerate), 100-101
Albania: Yugoslavian relations with, 60
Albanians: autonomy lost, 79; break with Stalin affecting, 58; demographic data, 17; designation as minority, 76, 122-23; as Kosovo minority, 36; Kosovo uprising, 65; in Montenegro and Macedonia, 164n; percentage of population, 15; self-determination denied to, 74; suppression of uprisings by, 54
Andric, Ivo, 39, 161n
Arkan. See Raznjatovic, Zeljko
Army: ethnic and political tradition in, 77; relationship to Serbia, 76-79; Serbian dominance in, 54, 55
Austro-Hungarian empire: ethnic exploitation in, 35

Badinter, Robert, 20, 121
Badinter Commission, 96, 121
Bakaric, Vladimir, 20, 52
Balance of trade. See Trade balance
Begic, Midhat, 106
Boban, Mate, 13, 20, 84, 95-96, 97, 104, 107, 108

Bosnia-Herzegovina: alternative policies for, 127; armed conflict and dismemberment of, 93-94; as "artificial" entity, 86-87; autonomous Croat regions in, 96; Bihac enclave, 100-101; city-countryside conflict in, 41; Croat-Muslim alliance, 102, 106-10; ethnic and social composition, 87-88; ethnic composition and religious affiliation in, 89; ethnic composition of, 19; "Herceg-Bosna" republic, 95, 96; international antagonism towards statehood for, 124-25; main periods in history of, 85-86; as multicultural country, 13-14; multiethnic resistance in, 103-4; Muslim nationalism in, 98-100; Muslims targeted in, 93-97; national communities in, 73-74; national groups' relationships in, 90-91; nationalist parties in, 81, 91-92; opposed logics within armed forces, 102; peace plans proposed for, 109-10; religion and national identity in, 39; religious stratification in, 87-88; religious tolerance and diversity in, 39-40; Serbian Gorazde offensive, 107-8; types of

municipalities in, 87; urbanization in, 41, 89-90; Vance-Owen Plan, 104-6; violation of integrity of, 119-20; World War II genocide in, 49; Yugoslavian disintegration and self-interest of, 72-73
Bosnians: ethnic and national differentiation among, 41
Bougarel, Xavier, 40, 87, 89, 90, 93

Capitalism: globalization, 112; instability and, 143; Yugoslavian investment, 114
Carter, Jimmy, 97
Catholic Church, 108
Cerovic, Stanko, 44
Chetniks, 48-49, 83, 132, 162n
Cicak, Ivan Zvonimir, 20, 79-80
Citizenship: nationality vs., 27-28; republican model of, 30
Civil society: oppression challenged by, 131
Clinton, Bill, 115
Collective rights, 140-42
Communist Party, 46, 52, 63, 164n; role during World War II, 49; second Yugoslavia and legitimation of, 57-58. *See also* Titoism
Cosic, Dobrica, 20
Croat Consultative Council, 107
Croatia: and Austro-Hungarian empire, 35; constitutional changes in, 79-80; definitions of "Croatness," 37; ethnic cleansing in, 84; ethnic composition of, 19; manipulation of nationalist sentiments in, 82-83; military intervention in, 76-78; Muslims' historical relationship with, 41-42; nationalities in, 73; parliamentary forms in, 84; self-determination question in, 74; Serbs as minority in, 35-36; sovereignty referendum in, 70; state and ethnicity in, 28; Titoism and, 53-55; Ustashe movement, 36, 48-49, 55, 83; Vance-Owen Plan, 104-6; Yugoslavian disintegration and self-interest of, 71-73
Croatian Spring, 53, 54, 163n
Croats: demographic data, 17; historically, 45-46; percentage of population, 15

Dalmatia, 37; Illyrian movement in, 44
Democracy: adequate forms of, 135-36; and collective rights, 140-42; peoples' rights, minority rights, and individual rights, 138-39; as regulator, 134-35; and right to self-determination, 136-38
Development Fund, 56
Displacement, 34
Dizdarevic, Svebor, 91
Djilas, Milovan, 20
Djuric, Yvan, 72, 76
Draskovic, Vuk, 20, 75

Economic policy: conditions during 1980s, 55-56; decentralization, 61-62; economic growth and growth of debt, 63; move toward recentralization, 63-64; "shock therapy," 64; Titoist economics affecting Croatia, 53-54; and world capitalist crisis, 112
Embargo policies, 127-28
Ethnic cleansing, 80, 105, 126; in Croatia, 84; displacement of refugees, 34; nation-state and,

27-28; during World War II, 48-50
Ethnicity: articulation of religion with, 38-39; in Bosnia-Herzegovina, 87-88; composition in Bosnia, 89; demographics, 15, 17; ethnic composition map, 18; ethnic composition of republics, 19; exploitation to divide and rule, 35; and nation-state, 27; thesis of "ethnically-based civil war," 120; urbanization and multiethnicity, 89-90
European Union, 56

Fascism: Bosnian resistance to, 86; extreme right-wing populism, 83-84; interethnic conflicts during World War II, 48-50; Jews and Croat fascists, 80; World War II resistance to, 132-33
Feron, Bernard, 32, 47
Fiser, Nenad, 41, 92
Foreign debt, 55, 56; growth of, 63
Foreign economic aid, 62
Foreign trade. *See* Trade balance
France: as republican model, 30-31
Free-market policies, 11; effects on Eastern Europe, 112-13
Free market policies: instability and, 143
Gautier, Xavier, 26
Germany, 113; Slovenian economic ties with, 56; state and ethnicity in, 27-28; and Yugoslavian fragmentation, 119
Gorazde: Serbian offensive against, 107-8
Greater Serbian project, 75-76
Gypsies. *See* Roma

Haveric, Tariq, 20, 102, 125
Homogeneity: ethnicity and nation-state and, 26-28
Horvat, Branko, 61, 77
Hungarians: demographic data, 17; percentage of population, 15
Hungary: minority rights in, 139-40
Hyperinflation, 55, 64

Illyrian movement, 44
Income: Slovenian per capita, 56
Independent Croat State, 36
Inflation, 55, 64
International Monetary Fund (IMF), 63, 64, 112
Islamic Declaration, 100
Israel: state and ethnicity in, 28
Ivekovic, Rada, 25, 84
Izetbegovic, Alija, 10, 12, 20-21, 94, 96, 98, 100, 101, 102, 103, 106, 125, 128, 131

Jews: and Croat fascists, 80; extermination during World War II, 49
Juppe, Alain, 109

Karadzic, Radovan, 13, 21, 92, 94, 95, 97, 101, 107, 109, 130
Kardelj, Edvard, 21, 52
Kljujic, Stjepan, 21, 96, 107
Knin Krajina, 36
Kosovo, 36; Albanian autonomy lost in, 79; demands for recognition of, 123; ethnic composition of, 19; as "internal Serbian affair," 81-82; name usage, 160$n$; repression of Albanians in, 58; uprisings in, 65. *See also* Albanians
Krleza, Miroslav, 26
Krulic, Joseph, 31, 36, 47

Kucan, Milan, 21, 74

Lacoste, Yves, 110
Language: codification of, 55; ethnic purging of, 26-27; and nationalistic considerations, 37-38; and Yugoslav state, 42-43
League of Yugoslav Communists, 63, 64, 89
LePen, Jean-Marie, 83, 142

Maastricht Treaty, 33, 34, 111, 114
Macedonia: Albanians in, 164$n$; ethnic composition of, 19; Macedonian nation, 170-71$n$; as nation, 38; Yugoslavian disintegration and self-interest of, 72-73
Macedonians: demographic data, 17; percentage of population, 15
Market: and economic decentralization, 61-62; as force for disintegration, 64-65; free-market policies, 11; Titoist economics affecting Croatia, 53-54
Markovic, Ante, 21, 29, 63, 64, 69, 74, 75, 77, 78, 89, 119
Matvejevic, Predrag, 47, 143
Media: obfuscation by, 9-10
Memorandum of the Serbian Academy of Sciences (1986), 75
Merlino, Jacques, 110
Mesic, Stipe, 21, 107
Mexico: national movements in, 141-42
Military: ethnic and political tradition in, 77; relationship to Serbia, 76-79; Serbian dominance in, 54, 55
Militias, 102; and Bosnian army, 94-95; Croatian, 94; Serbian right-wing, 75-76

Milosevic, Slobodan, 12, 21, 50, 64, 65, 66, 69, 72, 74, 75, 77, 78, 79, 83, 84, 92, 97, 108, 113, 114, 127, 164-65$n$
Mladic, Ratko, 21, 94, 108
Mocnik, Rastko, 59
Montenegrins: demographic data, 17; national identity of, 38; percentage of population, 15
Montenegro: Albanians in, 164$n$; ethnic composition of, 19; refugees in, 80; Yugoslavian disintegration and self-interest of, 72
Muslims: in Bosnia-Herzegovina, 88; and Bosnian statehood, 124-25; conversion in Bosnia-Herzegovina, 39; Croat-Muslim alliance, 102, 106-10; demographic data, 17; fundamentalism, 100, 169$n$; nationalism in Bosnia, 98-100; and Ottoman rule, 40; percentage of population, 15; right of self-defense, 128; secularization of, 43; Serb and Croat nationalism affecting, 41-42; targeted in Bosnia, 93-97; use of term, 161-62$n$

Napoleon, 44
*Narodnost*, 59-60
National Council of Serbs, Croats, and Slovenes, 46
Nationalism: Bosnian Muslim, 98-100; collective rights and, 140-42; and logic of territorial ownership, 35-37; manipulation of, 82; movements in opposition to, 131-32; Muslims and, 41; role in Yugoslav crisis, 29; Serbian roots of, 37
Nationality: and citizenship, 27-28;

# INDEX

minorities as "peoples," 122-24; minority rights, 121; minority status and, 73
National question: Titoism and, 42, 59-60
Nation-state: and context of Yugoslav breakup, 25-26; and ethnic cleansing, 27-28; profiting parties from building of, 71-73; types of, 27; war for purpose of building, 80; Yugoslavism and, 43
NATO, 126
Nedic, Milan, 21, 49
Nicolaidis, Dimitri, 26

Orthodox Church, 108, 130
Ottoman Empire: status of Serbs under, 39
Owen-Stoltenberg Plan, 105, 122
Ownership: logic of territorial, 35-37

Panic, Milan, 21-22, 78, 167*n*
Party of Right, 44
Party of Serb Renewal, 75
Pavelic, Ante, 22, 48
Peace plans, 116, 130-31
Populism: extreme right-wing, 83-84
Pupovac, Milorad, 82-83

Qosja, Rexhep, 123

Radical Party (Serbia), 75, 83
Rankovic, Aleksandr, 22, 54
Raznjatovic, Zeljko, 22, 94
Refugees, 34, 105, 109; nationality of, 80; western policies toward, 115
Religion: affiliations in Bosnia, 89; ethnicity and, 38-39; stratification in Bosnia-Herzegovina, 87-88; tolerance and diversity, 39-40
Right of separation: international community and, 121
Roma, 59, 136; extermination during World War II, 49; percentage of population, 15
Roux, Michel, 36
Rugovo, Ibrahim, 22

SDA (Muslim party), 98, 99, 101, 108
Self-determination: collective rights and, 140-42; as democratic right, 136-38; international community and right of, 121; and peoples' rights, minority rights, and individual rights, 138-39; of peoples vs. republics, 74-75, 122-24
Self-management programs, 61-62, 111
Serbia: army's relationship to, 76-79; constitutional changes in, 79-80; embargo affecting, 127-28; ethnic composition of, 19; Greater Serbian project, 75-76; minority provinces in, 73; notion of "Serbness," 37-38; offensive against Gorazde, 107-8; parliamentary forms in, 84; peace plans affecting, 130-31; refugees in, 80; responsibility for war, 80-81; restoration of domination by, 66; right-wing militias in, 75-76; roots of nationalism, 37; self-determination question in, 74; Titoism and, 52-53; Yugoslavian disintegration and pivotal role played by, 65-67;

Yugoslavian disintegration and self-interest of, 71-73
Serbo-Croatian (language), 26-27, 37-38, 42; administrative codification of, 55
Serbs: in Austro-Hungarian empire, 35; in Bosnia-Herzegovina, 87-88; demographic data, 17; as minority in Croatia, 35-36; percentage of population, 15; and South Slav emancipation, 45; status under Ottoman rule of, 39
Seselj, Vojislav, 22, 75, 78-79, 83, 92, 94
Silajdzic, Haris, 22
Slovenes: demographic data, 17; historical background, 45; percentage of population, 15
Slovenia: army's intervention in, 76, 77; economic conditions during 1980s, 55-56; ethnic composition of, 19; independence for, 70; self-determination question in, 74; Yugoslavian disintegration and self-interest of, 71-72
Slovenian Territorial Defense, 78
Socialist market: Titoist economics affecting Croatia, 53-54
Soviet Union: break with, 58; Slovenian trade with, 56
Stalinism, 54; Communist Party and, 58
Starcevic, Ante, 22, 44
Strikes, 63
Susak, Gojko, 22, 84, 94, 95

Territorial ownership: logic of, 35-37
Tito, Josip Broz, 22, 52
Titoism, 32; balance sheet, 51-67; contradictory aspects of, 58-62; from Croatian perspective, 53-55; disintegration of Yugoslavia, 65-67; economic conditions during 1980s, 55-56; economic decentralization under, 61-62; key dates, 51; legitimation of Communist Party, 57-58; Muslims and, 42; and national question, 42, 59-60; and national recognition, 38; 1980s crisis, 62-67; and partisan tradition, 167$n$; relation of republics to federal center, 60; from Serbian perspective, 52-53; Serbian sovereignty under, 79; and Soviet threat, 165$n$; Stalinism, 54
Tourism: in Croatia, 54
Trade balance, 55; German-Slovenian, 56
Treaty of Lausanne (1923), 26
Trumbic, Ante, 23, 46
Tudjman, Franjo, 10, 13, 23, 37, 51, 69, 70, 82, 84, 94, 95, 96, 97, 104, 106, 107, 113, 120, 127

Unemployment: in Kosovo, 65
United Nations: mandate of, 126
United States: contradictory policies of, 115; republican model of citizenship, 30; strategic goals of, 126-27
Urbanization: in Bosnia, 41, 89-90
Useljenicki, Bogdan, 102, 103
Ustashe movement, 36, 48-49, 55, 83

Vance-Owen Plan, 104-6, 125
Varady, Tibor, 133
Voivodina: ethnic composition of, 19

# INDEX

Wages: work and, 53-54
War: and building of nation-state, 80; joint but unequal responsibilities for, 81-83; Serbian responsibility in, 80-81
Wieviorka, Michel, 141
Women: nationalist "reconquest" of, 84; rape, 165*n*
Workers: self-management programs, 61-62, 111; strikes, 63
World War II: antifascist resistance during, 132-33; interethnic conflicts during, 48-50

Yugoslavia: "artificiality" of second state, 57-58; breakup in historical context, 25-26; Croat-Serb coalition in Zagreb Diet (1906-1918), 44; democracy lacking in, 134-35; dependence on foreign capital before World War II, 47-48; disparities between republics, 68; economic conditions during 1980s, 55-56; ethnic composition map, 18; ethnic composition of republics, 19; ethnic identification in, 28; ethnicity demographics, 15, 17; failure of first state, 46-47; foreign economic aid to, 62; founding of, 25; general map of, 16; glossary of names, 20-23; interethnic conflicts during World War II, 48-50; international community and right of separation, 121; key historical dates, 24; language and, 42-43; loss of strategic importance, 113-14; overview of crisis, 25-34; peace plans, 116; post-World War I union, 44-45; pragmatism on national questions, 59-60; Serbian pivotal role in disintegration of, 65-67; socioeconomic crisis and fragmentation of, 32-33; violation of integrity of, 119; war's motive force in, 11. *See also individual republics*; Titoism
"Yugoslavism," 25, 29; main objectives of, 66-67; as threat to particular identities, 159-60*n*. *See also* Titoism
"Yugoslavs": percentage of population, 15

Zagreb Diet (1906-1918): Croat-Serb coalition in, 44